VETERAN'S NOTES
BLOGGERY OF AN IRAQ WAR VET

SCOTT ALBRIGHT

ISBN: 148029487X
ISBN-13: 978-1480294875

DEDICATION

Veteran's Notes is dedicated to the men and women who have put on a uniform to fight in the name of their country, religion, or ideology only to find out after taking off the uniform that the violence and warfare was never necessary. This is for those men and women who, despite being intimidated, bullied, and punished by the very same people they fought for, broke the silence and spoke out against the senseless killing.

This is for those who have been to war and who understand just how awful it is and who have done what they can to change the course of history. This is also for those men and women still in uniform who every day deal with the moral dilemma of having to choose between taking lives or saving lives on a continuous basis.

Finally, this is for all the military veterans in the United States who have sacrificed their time, energy, and even their lives to provide what they believe is a service to their community and country. Those sacrifices will not be forgotten and hopefully are not all made in vain. Despite the tragic violence that has occurred because of U.S. military policy, real advancements have been made in the area of international security that do make the world a safer and more peaceful place for people across the globe. Thank you for your service and sacrifices!

ACKNOWLEDGMENTS

The former owner and publisher of *The Independent* newspaper, Wally Gordon, was instrumental in providing me the opportunity to write and report on veterans' issues. He cannot be thanked enough for allowing me to republish my work on my website and blog while working at the paper. Leota Harriman, the current publisher and part-owner of *The Independent,* was also generous enough to allow me to reprint many of the articles published in the newspaper here in this book. Thank you Wally and Leota for your support and guidance. *Veteran's Notes* would not exist without either of you. A special thanks also goes out to my dad, Rick Albright, for his contributions to this book, and for his service as a veteran, teacher, mentor, and father. Thanks dad.

CONTENTS

Preparing for war. Northern Kuwait, March 2003.

INTRODUCTION

Welcome to the print edition of *Veteran's Notes: Bloggery of an Iraq War Vet.* In this edition you'll find a new contribution by my father, Rick Albright, a Vietnam war vet and retired teacher who tells the story of his return to Vietnam some forty-two years after first visiting the country as a U.S. Marine. Also exclusively included in this print edition is an article originally written for *The Independent* about PTSD which, thanks to reader feedback, became a printed forum discussing the media's role in detailing the more gruesome aspects of war in public spaces. Additional notes are added to this post explaining why I think much of the mainstream media missed seeing a huge amount of those not-so-nice aspects of the war during the assault on al-Nasiriyah. These notes, combined with the other commentary scattered throughout this book, provide a new contribution to the available literature and ongoing dialogue on veterans' issues and U.S. wartime policies. Additionally, this book has many useful references and citations for researchers, scholars, military recruits, active duty military, and veterans seeking to find more information about the related material. This book is suited for many settings and can be used as reference material for a school assignment or research project, in the classroom as a learning tool, at home for pleasure reading, or in a number of other places where there is an interest in reading about the wars in Iraq and Afghanistan and how returning soldiers have been affected by those wars.

So what exactly is *Veteran's Notes* about you ask? Well, it's about many things, but mostly it's my story about returning home from war and the reflections I've had about veterans issues and other current events. More precisely, it's a collection of notes, thoughts, poems, essays, newspaper articles, and blog posts written by me, Scott Albright, a veteran of the Iraq War and survivor of the aftermath. No, these are not stories about my experience in the war, but rather the stories of my experience as a veteran and reporter after coming home from the war. That "war story" will be told sometime later in the future when I'm able to assess the experience from a wiser and more academic perspective.

It was just ten crazy years ago that I was sent to Iraq in the March 2003 invasion of the country, where I served as a machine gunner with Bravo Company 1/4, First Marine Division. After spending about five months in country during the invasion and initial post-invasion security operations, I returned to Camp Pendleton, California before I was once again deployed to Iraq where I spent three months in Fallujah getting sniped at and mortared fairly regularly. After returning the States I exited the military and returned to civilian life in my hometown of Albuquerque, New Mexico.

Back home I became engaged in my college studies, receiving a Bachelor of Arts degree in political science at the University of New Mexico in the summer of 2007. After working a few different jobs in Albuquerque and Northern New Mexico, I eventually found a good gig at The Independent in Edgewood, where I would work until I moved to Hilo, Hawaiʻi in December 2009. I received a Master of Arts degree in China-U.S. Relations at the University of Hawaiʻi at Hilo.

While in Hawaii I continued developing the website and blog I had begun in New Mexico while working at *The Independent.* I changed the name of the website, theworldsword.com, to chinausrelations.com, and the blog, iraqwarvets.blogspot.com, to militarytalkshop.blogspot.com. The following book is a compilation of the works I have done on veteran and military issues on these sites and elsewhere. Although links have been converted to citations, and some spelling, grammar, and style changes have been made in addition to a few side notes being added, the majority of the posts and articles printed here remain in their original format. Most of the posts printed here have been removed from Military Talk Shop and cannot be found anywhere else, making this a truly unique reading experience.

Because you have opted to purchase the print version of *Veteran's Notes* instead of the digital version, I removed most of the pictures that are in the digital version and am printing in black and white to keep the cost to you as low as possible. To purchase a color digital edition of *Veterans Notes* visit: http://www.amazon.com/dp/B00A5ER67Q or check out http://www.veteransnotes.weebly.com.

If you have any concerns, questions, or comments please contact me at albright.scott@gmail.com. Thanks, and enjoy the bloggery!

Mon Mar 4, 2013 | 5:37 PM

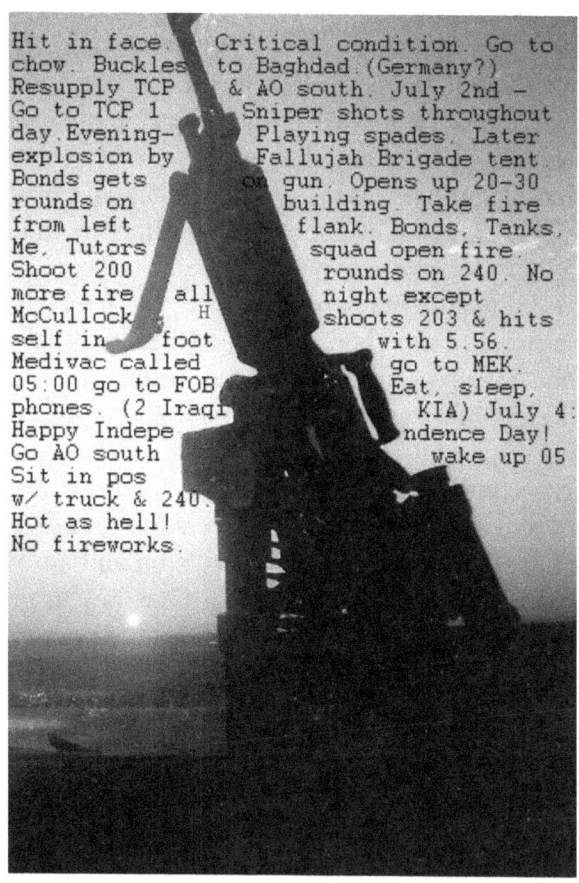

Hit in face. Critical condition. Go to
chow. Buckles to Baghdad (Germany?)
Resupply TCP & AO south. July 2nd —
Go to TCP 1 Sniper shots throughout
day. Evening— Playing spades. Later
explosion by Fallujah Brigade tent.
Bonds gets on gun. Opens up 20-30
rounds on building. Take fire
from left flank. Bonds, Tanks,
Me. Tutors squad open fire.
Shoot 200 rounds on 240. No
more fire all night except
McCullock H shoots 203 & hits
self in foot with 5.56.
Medivac called go to MEK.
05:00 go to FOB Eat, sleep.
phones. (2 Iraqi KIA) July 4:
Happy Indepe ndence Day!
Go AO south wake up 05
Sit in pos
w/ truck & 240.
Hot as hell!
No fireworks.

1| MORAL DILEMMAS

Joining the Military

I was listening to a talk show radio program that featured two sergeants discussing the war in Iraq and PTSD when a caller asked what she could do to inform her 17-year-old son about the military, as he said he is going to join as soon as he is of age. I thought about calling but didn't. I wanted to tell this lady that there isn't anything she can do to stop her son from joining, but she can tell him some things I wish I would have known.

The Marine Corps was intriguing to me because of the glamour that is portrayed in recruiting videos and in movies. It is a place that will make a man out of you and teach you discipline. It is a line of work where you can save lives and get the bad guys. I was drawn to this because I wanted to be a better person and I thought the Marines would do this for me. The truth is nobody can make you a better person but yourself. There are druggies and drunks, and racists and creeps and assholes in the military, just like every other place on earth. When I realized this I became disappointed and fell into some bad behavior which I now regret. I thought the Marines would make me this great person that we read about in the papers, but I finally realized that it was never the Marines that made those people great, it was their heart and soul. It is their courage and state of mind, their persistence and internal strength. It is not something that you can be trained to be. It comes from within and you can be this person in any line of work. You can be a hero working at McDonalds or in a factory, you can change lives for the better just about anywhere, including your own. I wish I would have known this because I think I would have been a better Marine and would have had the courage to stop some of the senseless killing that even the highest ranking officials didn't stop.

I believe that there are leaders in the U.S. military that have this courage but there are far too few of them and many are shut out by the cowards who feel like they can win wars through fear and violence. If I could say anything to that 17-year-old I would say go ahead and join, but do it for the right reasons and don't give up.
Fri Aug 1, 2008 | 07:06 PM |

What's the Solution?
What can be done to help facilitate the needs of veterans returning home from Iraq and Afghanistan? Everyone please comment here. Send all viable solutions to your local government representatives or future representatives. One solution is the veteran's court in Buffalo, New York which helps keep veterans out of jail for nonviolent crimes.
Sat Aug 9, 2008 | 08:29 PM |

Moral Killing

One of the hardest things about returning home from a combat zone is coming to the realization that the rules have changed. Figuring out what is right and what is wrong isn't as easy as reading the federal and state laws. Morals and values are different in garrison than in war. Killing is no longer acceptable. It was okay in combat when there was a positively identified enemy combatant. You get an award if you kill the bad guy. Killing women and children isn't okay, even if the women and children are supplying food, weapons and intelligence to the guy shooting at you. Back home all killing is wrong, except for maybe an unborn child in some states. Killing an animal is okay if you have a license and it is hunting season or you work on a farm or in a slaughter house. Raising the animal to fight another animal is not okay, but training humans to beat the crap out of another human is perfectly fine and its even shown on television so anybody can watch. In fact violence on TV is more okay than sex. Of course this doesn't mean the act of loving another person physically is worse than beating someone, it's just morally correct to not televise the act of loving. Of course if one shows sexual love towards a minor this is the most evil of all sins, even more so than beating a child. It's okay for a 40-year-old to have sex with a 30-year-old, but it's not okay for an 18-year-old to have sex with a 16-year-old.

A 16-year-old may or may not be treated as an adult by the legal system for certain crimes, but they can never buy cigarettes or alcohol. Alcohol and cigarettes contribute to more deaths than marijuana, but smoking a joint can ruin a career, but being a drunk will only require treatment of some kind buy many employers. An employer can of course overwork and underpay an employee but employees cannot take home a pencil or pen from work as that is considered stealing. The government can bill you for a trip to the ambulance if a cop storms into your house and tasers you, but if a regular every day Joe walks into someone else's house, beats them and then drives them to the hospital and asks for money for the ride a whole assortment of charges will be given to the person doing the beating. Of course beating someone up is a show of strength and manliness but walking away from a fight is shown as a sign of cowardice.

As an infantryman I could never pick or choose my fights but as a civilian if myself and a hundred other guys are told to fight another group and we do so without question this will probably be considered a gang fight. Those who order soldiers into battle usually do not fight themselves but if a civilian orders others to fight without doing so as well it is looked down upon by authorities as well as those who are fighting, unless it is the owner of the UFC or some other similar organization.

All these things get mixed and mashed in my head when trying to figure out what the best thing to do is under every circumstance. I'm sure there is a clear right and wrong but I am even surer it is not written in man's laws. The morals we are taught to live by each day don't make much sense when you put them all together, but when looking within I know deep inside that I will do the right thing when tested. Now I must ask myself, have our leaders done the right thing?[1]
Mon Aug 11, 2008 | 08:03 PM |

After Note: As a student of political science I am familiar with just war doctrine and have come to realize that no matter where I am in the world people will always find a justification for using violence, no matter how irrational that justification is. The U.S. is not the only country in the world that follows such a doctrine, nor is it the only nation which follows a policy of exceptionalism through physical and ideological expansionism. Just as some people in the U.S. believe it is manifest destiny for the rest of the world to succumb to the American way of life, many Chinese people believe the CCP is justified in their actions through the mandate of heaven. If two sides believe they are waging war for just causes then the violence both sides engage in must be morally acceptable right? NO WAY! It's time to re-think how nations justify their use of violence so future generations aren't tricked into believing war is just, good, or inevitable, because it's not. The use of violence to obtain specific objectives is no longer an acceptable practice for individuals, corporations, nations, or any other such entity.

Russia and the U.S.
Did the Cold War really end? I don't think so. Look at Iraq, Afghanistan, Iran, Syria, Israel, Peru, Chile, Colombia, Venezuela and so many more places around the globe and look at who is allied with who and who has weapons from where.[2] Yes sir! The weapons trade didn't end with the fall of the Soviet Union. The U.S. and Russia have been neck to neck in the race against who can build the biggest most deadliest bomb for decades. The recent event in Georgia is only a continuation of a long back and forth battle between the U.S. and Russia's struggle for power across the globe. Perhaps there are more players now with more objectives and goals, but the two weapons building power states are still in the game and still playing dirty.

Who's behind this turf war? The Russian Mafia? Skulls and Bones? The Illuminati? Militaries? Corporations? All of them, or nobody at all? Maybe it's just taken its own course with no one really behind the reins, but it sure hasn't come to a halt. And it's frightening as all hell. Talk about PTSD syndromes. This whole idea of mutually assured destruction should have us all jumping under tables with every ring of a school bell. Maybe people have just become so accustomed to the idea that we're just mortal men and women who die anyway, that the thought of a nuclear holocaust isn't so bad. Well whatever the case may be it seems pretty screwy. I'm hoping that it's just a conspiracy to wipe out humans by the insects who are brainwashing us at night with their constant cricking. At least if I know the insects are behind this I won't feel too bad being wiped out by a Russian nuke. They probably just had a bad infestation this year.

After Note: Somehow I deleted the date for this post and can't find it on my computer. The funny thing about this post is that I don't even remember being too bothered by any insects while in New Mexico, but now that I'm in Hawai'i, I am constantly bugged by the annoying coqui frogs every night. I can't even hear myself think sometimes, and my wife has even commented that its probably just a ploy by the military to cover the noises created during all the military testing they do here. Well it'd be a great cover anyway.

Injured Vets
To learn about Cpl. Jason Poole, a fellow Marine who served in my unit and who was hit by an IED check out the film *Going the Distance*, a documentary about traumatic brain injury. Information about the film can be found at the Going the Distance website.[3]
Wed Sep 10, 2008 | 08:29 AM |

After Note: I added the Going the Distance link November 11, 2012. It is a website about a an hour long television documentary on survivors of traumatic brain injury. When I visited the website and saw Poole's picture I suddenly felt sick. What a messed up thing to have happened to him. What a messed up war!

Welcome Back Veterans

To all those who just returned: Welcome Home! For those of us who have been back awhile: Don't you love being home? Well it can be a bit crazy, even after two, three or even four years after getting out. Things are different now and it's not easy to accept. A few years ago I was charged with guarding equipment worth hundreds of thousands of dollars and was given the authority to shoot to kill if anyone tried to steal it. The jobs we had overseas often times don't compare to what we're offered here, but I've found that it's okay. People don't understand how demanding our jobs were and they don't care how important we were then. I've learned to accept the fact that people don't think I can handle certain tasks. Let them be blind, even if it means taking on seemingly meaningless tasks. Living simple like isn't so bad.

War on Terror

Terrorists, insurgents, mercenaries, gangsters, thugs, hoodlums and regular every day criminals were the enemy in Iraq. I was trained to fight and kill whomever was labeled as such. It didn't matter where they were from or what religion they were. If I was shot at I could shoot back. While in Iraq we detained Syrians, Jordanians, Egyptians and even dealt with the mercenaries from the French Foreign Legion. Over there it was okay to protect myself against gun runners, bomb makers, suicide attackers and the like, but back home that's a no-no. As I am no longer employed in the security services I have given up my right to protect myself against gangsters in my own city. There are drive-byes, murders, robberies, gang brawls, and other such activities going on where I live but I am no longer involved in trying to stop these type of things from taking place. It is difficult at times because I feel hypersensitive to my surroundings and when danger is lurking I have a desire to seek it. Instead I must go indoors or relocate but the anxiety of knowing something bad is taking place doesn't stop. I am paranoid at times thinking I am a possible target for these hoodlums. I have come to believe that we live in a society where it truly is us against them, but I am neither us nor them anymore.

Terrorism is not just something that comes from the Middle East. It is all around me. I see it in government, in the military, in corporations, and in the streets. The United States has lost face in this war and has cracked down on whoever it decides is the terrorist for the day, losing potential allies along the way. This week Sunni's, the next it's week Shiites. Perhaps will get the ex Marine tomorrow. I'm truly frightened of this war where anyone can get locked up, shot, or tasered for just about anything if labeled as "them". America has plopped her troops in one region to fight this war when it is a worldwide phenomenon. Terrorists hide in every crook and cranny on this planet, yet they walk free while the United States creates more angry mobs in Afghanistan and Iraq. This war has made me feel less safe than before. Both presidential nominees have it wrong. We don't need to stay in Iraq or Afghanistan; we need to refocus military operations in different parts of the world, putting an emphasis on prevention and rehabilitation. Now that the U.S. has committed itself to being the world's police it should reexamine what needs to be done and who should be considered an ally and who should be considered a foe. The war on terror is not a war on Arabs or Muslims; it is a war on international criminal networks seeking to cause pain, misery and mayhem to anyone and everyone, and should be fought as such.

Mon Oct 6, 2008 | 08:33 PM |

Military Service Counts as Work Experience

"Don't expect anything from anybody when you get out."

That's what Gunny Mo used to tell us back at Camp Pendleton. He said not to expect a pat on the back, a thank you or even a free beer when we became civilians. Of course I had seen the videos of how Vietnam veterans were treated after their war, but I was pretty sure things would be better for me. And they have been. As an Iraq war veteran I did receive a nice welcome home and even a few free beers, but it still hasn't been easy. This Veteran's Day I'd like to remind everyone about the difficulty all veterans face when transitioning from the military to civilian life.

Plenty of times I've seen someone on the side of a freeway off ramp with a sign saying homeless vet, but I never felt sorry for them. I always thought that anybody can make it in America and that a job is easy to come by, especially for vets. Well I've found that that's not exactly true. Unemployment is plaguing the country, the economy is on a roller coaster, America is engaged in two wars and the affects of it all are especially hard on veterans.

Every so often I go to the vet center in Albuquerque where I talk to old Marines, squids and soldiers. Many of them have PTSD, amongst other disabilities, and are struggling to deal with life as a civilian. One of the topics we've discussed is working while collecting disability. I heard one of the guys say they could work as long as they lied about what medication they were taking. Others have said they just couldn't get hired because of their service connected disability. For me it hasn't been so hard getting a job, as it has been dealing with the fact that no job feels quite as important as the one I had as a Marine. As a Marine I had the responsibility of having to choose whether to take a life or to save a life on a regular basis. Nothing can feel quite as a great as knowing you can change someone's future so much.

My dad, who is also in ex-Marine, explained that employers don't understand that this is a job skill and counts as work experience. He said employers see 23-year-old men and women fresh out of the service as though they are just starting life. "No matter what job I do I always feel like I am 4 years behind my peers," my dad said.

I tend to believe him because my friends who didn't join the service are much further along in their careers than myself and the Marines who got out around the same time as me are. For those of us who were in the infantry it's been even harder to find jobs where our military training transfers over into the civilian sector.[4] A couple guys I served with joined Blackwater, one of my good friends joined the reserves to go back to Iraq for what he called a vacation from the civilian world, and another one of my friends is collecting disability and going to school. My old sergeant wrote me and said he was turned down from the New York Police Department because he couldn't pass the mental exam and is back to the same job he had before the Marines, and another guy I served with is working at Walgreens. There's nothing wrong with any of these jobs, because as my grandpa, also a veteran, said, "A job doesn't bring you dignity, you bring dignity to the job," but I still have a hard time thinking about my friend who was once in charge of guarding thousands of dollars worth of high tech equipment working at Walgreens as a cashier.

Both my dad and I agreed that it us up to the individual as to how they want to use their military training in the civilian world, but I still wonder if there are vets out there who just can't convince employers that their military experience does count in the civilian sector. For all those who served thank you, and for all those considering hiring a vet, remember running a squad or a platoon counts as managerial skills, being able to monitor a radio and call in air support counts as communication skills and firing a weapon in combat counts as critical decision making skills. Happy Veteran's Day!

Tue Nov 11, 2008 | 09:13 AM |

CHAPTER 1 NOTES

[1] Suggested reading: McKeogh, Colm. *Innocent Civilians: The Morality of Killing in War.* New York: Palgrave, 2002.

[2] See Grimmet, Richard F. and Paul K. Kerr. "Conventional Arms Transfers to Developing Nations, 2004-2011," August 24, 2012. http://www.fas.org/sgp/crs/weapons/R42678.pdf.

[3] See http://www.goingthedistance.info/film.html.

[4] For resources on how military skills transfer into the civilian sector and for a list of some good employment services for veterans see the Iraq and Afghanistan Veteran's of America website at http://iava.org/resources/category/5.

2| HOLIDAY SPIRIT

A Soldier's Christmas away from Home
First published in *The Independent* newspaper.[1]

Army Specialist Dustin Newsom, an Estancia High School graduate, won't be spending the holidays with his family this year. Newsom will be on a 48-hour mission in Mosul, Iraq starting Christmas day.

Newsom graduated from Estancia in 2003 and joined the Army in July 2006. He deployed to Iraq in December 2007, where he is a tank driver. He has only been home once since his 15-month deployment began.

Newsom's mother, Julie Griffo, who works for the Estancia School District, said she will wait until her son returns in February to celebrate Christmas.

"It's really hard to get in the Christmas spirit," Griffo said. "I know Christmas is important because it is the celebration of Christ's birthday, but it is hard to get in the spirit."

Griffo said she is grateful for the people in the community who ask about her son and appreciates the support they are giving her. She uses prayer to help manage the stress that comes with knowing her child is in a combat zone.

"I pray a lot," Griffo said. "I know God is watching over him. I don't know how parents that don't have a faith in God can handle it. That's the only thing that has kept me strong."

In an e-mail from Iraq, Newsom answered the question of what he wants the most for Christmas: "I have the best wife, family and friends anyone could ask for so I don't want anything except to be home."

Griffo's Christmas wish is the same: "What I would like most this Christmas would be for Dustin to be here – safe and sound. If that's not possible, a call from him would be great."

Although Newsom may not be able to call on Christmas day, his mother's wish to get a phone call sometime over the holidays may come true. In Newsom's e-mail he wrote, "We run our missions out of a small base in the city that has Internet and phone access so I can communicate with loved ones. Thank god."

When asked what the Iraqis think of the Christmas holiday, Newsom said some of the Iraqis he has met are Christians, but most of the communication he has with them is "usually directed toward more mission effectiveness."

Both Newsom's mother and wife, Danielle, sent care packages to Newsom for the holidays. Newsom did not say in his e-mail if he had received the packages.

Griffo still has fresh memories of celebrating the holidays with her son in previous years: "I have many great memories of Christmases past that I've been thinking about," Griffo said. "I like to remember us decorating cookies and making cinnamon wreath together, as well as going to Christmas Eve services at the Methodist church here in town. The service last year, right before Dustin deployed, was especially nice since both he and Danielle were there."

Several other locals have deployed overseas who won't be celebrating the holidays at home, including Dolores Delgado, one of Newsom's Estancia High School classmates.

Griffo explained how she found out that Delgado was in the same city as her son after talking to Delgado's mother, Barbara Delgado. Griffo said she was talking to Barbara Delgado one day when she said that her daughter had seen Newsom.

"I thought it was funny how her mom said Dolores saw Dustin," Griffo said. "I asked how she could recognize him out there because everybody looks the same. Dolores said she knew him by his walk."

Newsom and Delgado are not the only locals who will be spending their holidays in combat zones this year. Thirty-seven year old Tamara Mendez of Estancia will be spending the holidays in Kuwait where she provides landing coordinates for pilots. Her son Chris Mendez, a ninth grader at Estancia High School, said this is the first Christmas he'll spend without his mother around. Chris, who is also a cousin to Dolores Delgado, said the last time he spoke to his mother was about two months ago. He said he sent care packages to both his mother and cousin which included cookies, popcorn, books and magazines. He said the hardest thing about having his mom overseas is that he can talk to her but can't see her in person.

There is a benefit to his mom not being around for the holidays though.

"If I get a check or money I actually get to keep it instead of her giving it to my grandma," Chris said.

Chris said he's not too worried about his mom being in danger.

"She told me in the last letter that she was far away from the action."

Chris said that he has thought about joining the Marines because "they are the devil dogs. They're the ones that go in first for all the action."

He said if he does join he wants to be a sniper because he likes to hunt and is good with rifles.

According to Ray Seva, public information officer for the New Mexico Department of Veterans' Services, 1,506 New Mexicans are currently deployed in Iraq or Afghanistan. He said a total of 30,000 New Mexicans have served in one of those two countries since 2001.

Mon Dec 29, 2008 | 09:25 AM |

1,200 Care Packages Sent to Troops

First published in *The Independent* newspaper.

Blue Star Mothers, a volunteer organization established during the First World War to help support the war effort, sent out over 1,200 care packages to armed servicemen and women all over the world for the holidays. In the East Mountains, volunteers have worked together for the last two months getting packages together so those serving overseas can have a Christmas of their own.

Blue Stars is also involved in the Wounded Warrior and Walking Tall projects. For the Wounded Warrior project, volunteers send quilts, white t-shirts, underwear, socks and toiletries to soldiers who have been injured while serving in the military. The packages are sent to military hospitals in the U.S., Iraq and Germany. Over 249 quilts were sent this year, with more on the way.

For the Walking Tall project volunteers knit and crochet scarves and other items to give to orphan children in

Afghanistan. Hiltrud Ridenour, a Blue Star volunteer, said the gifts help to break the ice in tribal areas of Afghanistan where elders are skeptical of foreign soldiers.

"They are given a kinder reception," Ridenour said of the Americans who pass out the knitted items.

Ridenour said the packages sent to deployed soldiers were filled with goodies like hot chocolate, microwave popcorn, candy, and of course, green chile. The soldiers are also sent crossword puzzles, toothbrushes, disposable razors, wet wipes and other toiletry items.

"Everything is in small traveling sizes," Ridenour said, "so they can carry it with them on a mission."

This year volunteers made snowmen out of socks and wash cloths to give the troops a taste of the holidays. Ridenour said most of the boxes were sent to Iraq and Afghanistan but some were sent to South America, Africa and other parts of the world including Korea, where Ridenour's son is currently stationed.

Ridenour said the soldiers have been grateful for the packages and have written many thank you letters including one which came from a chaplain who said without the packages the Marines he is serving with would not have had a Christmas this year.

Blue Star Mothers will be mailing more packages out for Valentine's Day. Volunteers will meet toward the end of January to start packing boxes. For more information call Ridenour at 865-4240 or visit bluestarmoms.org.

Food and toiletry items can be delivered in person at 2919 2nd Street in Albuquerque. Monetary donations are always in need to help pay for shipping costs.

Mon Dec 29, 2008 | 09:31 AM |

Radical Islamic Terrorists vs. Extreme Right Wing Military Industrialists

Who is more extreme: Rush Limbaugh or Muqtada al Sadr? You might say Sadr because he is known for his calls for violence against the United States, but is his ideology that more extreme than someone like Rush? To me it seems ridiculous that the United States can call al Qaeda extreme in any way when the United States' military actions against terrorists is far more extreme than anything I've seen the terrorists do. Sure, bombing the USS Cole, the embassies in Kenya and Tanzania, 9/11 and other attacks are pretty far out there. I mean that's definitely more extreme than jumping off a helicopter with a snowboard strapped to your feet, but compared to a full out invasion on Iraq and Afghanistan an IED here and there is nothing.

Looking back over the short period of American history one could easily say the United States has used extreme measures to accomplish goals on many, many more occasions than the long history of Islamic "radicals". The use of the atomic bomb during WWII, the extreme violence of the Korean war, the death and destruction that came with the Vietnam war, the pure devastation that came with the Gulf War and the many, many proxy wars fought in Africa and South and Central America are just a few examples of how the United States has gone out of its way to ensure it is not using acceptable international norms to resolve conflicts. The norm really is peace, not retaliatory action, pre-emptive strikes or intimidation through military might.

The U.S. is one of very few countries who actually go to these extremes to resolve "threats to national security" or other so called conflicts of U.S. interest. But now it's gone a little too far. People across the world have seen that it takes extreme measures to answer to extreme forces and that is exactly what has happened in Israel and Gaza, and that's scary as hell. It's scary because extremism is spreading like a nasty disease. I look at all the comments on news articles about the war in Gaza and all I see are extreme idiots bragging about how one side will wipe out the other. The Zionist pigs vs. the rag-head bombers: That sounds like a comic book or something. And where are the moderates, the ones who used to be the norm? They can't be heard anymore so they either join one extreme group or just stay out of the fight. And that's what's scary. Everyone wants to jump behind a Rush Limbaugh or a Muqtada al Sadr and scream out how righteous they are. Well I'm personally going to sit on the fence and watch the extremists wear themselves out. Seriously, think of how much energy they expend trying to be far right or radically different. I think it's hard enough just trying to be normal. Well good luck with all your extremism. I think I'll just stick to the snowboarding

Mon Jan 12, 2009 | 11:02 AM |

After Thought: It has been reported that the U.S. has provided aid to Islamic extremists fighting against Bashar al-Assad's forces in the ongoing civil war in Syria.[2] Extreme is all relative I guess.

Marijuana for PTSD

A couple things to note: The state of New Mexico department of health has initiated the first step in getting marijuana legalized for patients suffering from PTSD. The marijuana advisory board approved:
Post Traumatic Stress Disorder, Peripheral neuropathy, Caxechia and wasting syndrome, Intractable nausea, Hepatitis

C under treatment (*not* "blanket" hepatitis C), Inflammatory Bowel Disease/Chron's disease, Fibromyalgia, ALS (aka Lou Gehrig's Disease),

The Board denied: Environmental Illness, Brain Dysfunction, Estrogen Replacement, Therapy, Depression, "Blanket" Hepatitis C

The Board tabled: Chronic Sinus Congestion from Blunt Facial Trauma, Bipolar disorder, Chronic Pain, Arthritis, Chronic Fatigue Syndrome, Asthma/COPD

Marijuana can already be used by patients suffering from "debilitating medical conditions." Debilitating medical condition means:

(1) cancer; (2) glaucoma; (3) multiple sclerosis; (4) damage to the nervous tissue of the spinal cord, with objective neurological indication of intractable spasticity; (5) epilepsy; (6) positive status for human immunodeficiency virus or acquired immune deficiency syndrome; (7) admitted into hospice care in accordance with rules promulgated by the department; or (8) any other medical condition, medical treatment or disease as *approved by the department*; and (9) which results in pain, suffering or debility for which there is credible evidence that medical use marijuana could be of benefit.

F. "Department" means the department of health. "Advisory board" means the medical marijuana advisory board consisting of eight (8) practitioners representing the fields of but not limited to neurology, pain management, medical oncology, psychiatry, infectious disease, family medicine and gynecology.[3]

From my understanding the board makes the recommendations to the department which than gives a final approval. From the reading of the statute it looks like once the department approves it, marijuana can then be used by patients suffering from the new listed conditions without any other approval except for a prescription from a doctor licensed to prescribe marijuana. Patients can apply to produce their own marijuana for personal use.

THIS IS A GREAT VICTORY FOR VETERANS WITH PTSD! FIND A DOCTOR LICENSED TO PRESCRIBE MARIJUANA AND GO GET A PRESCRIPTION! STOP TAKING TRAZADONE AND OTHER MEDICATIONS PRESCRIBED BY THE VA YOU DON'T NEED. MARIJUANA IS MILDER AND SAFER. AND IT WORKS!

Thu Jan 29, 2009 | 05:24 PM |

After Note: The *Huffington Post* reports that a psychologist is trying to remove PTSD from the list of medical conditions marijuana can be prescribed for in the state of New Mexico.[4] The article says a significant amount of those prescribed marijuana in New Mexico are veterans. During the November 6, 2012 election Washington and Colorado voted to legalize marijuana for recreational use. The federal government will presumably try to block this, but it seems to me that eventually the government will have to concede to the people and agree that either marijuana has legitimate medical uses, or accept that those who smoke marijuana for recreational purposes should not be treated like criminals. In my opinion there is very little difference between someone who drinks a couple beers after work to unwind and someone who takes a couple tokes of pot after work to unwind. One of the differences though is that I think the pot smoker is probably less of a threat to society for just smoking pot than the person who is just drinking a couple of beers. This is just from my own experiences in life, but from what I've seen pot smokers tend to commit fewer crimes and create less havoc in general than drinkers.

Military & School Set Me Eight Years Back

Had I not joined the military or gone to school I would probably be making a lot more money right now, with less stress, less frustrations and more pride in my country. . .
Unfortunately I made a huge mistake and joined the service in order to better myself and to do something for my country. What I did for my country is I helped in the invasion of Iraq - how that's bettered my country I'm still not sure. But perhaps the military did help me to better myself. I was taught to do whatever it takes and to not give up. And hopefully I won't forget that because I need to be a persistent son of a bitch to make it all pay off now.

Four years of being a grunt didn't help any in terms of getting experience in the workforce. There's just not much in the civilian sector for a machine gunner. So I took on the task of earning a degree to help me get my foot in the door. Well that was a mistake because I went for the one type of degree that just doesn't pay off unless you know someone in the field, you are wealthy enough to buy your way into the field, or you go on to get a masters or doctorate.

That's right; I got my degree in politics. And in New Mexico it's all politics. The state's VA office denied my vocation rehabilitation entitlement because I have too much education, I can't find a job in politics because I don't have enough education, the school denied me entrance into the graduate program because I'm not a good enough candidate and much of the other jobs I am capable of doing won't hire me because I'm overqualified.

So I've stepped back to get another perspective on the situation only to find out that I'm eight years behind my peers who decided to go to work straight out of high school. They have good high paying jobs, own their homes and have a couple years experience as a father or husband. Talk about keeping up with the Jones's! I thought the military and a good college education would set me out in front of the Jones's. Shit was I wrong.

As it turns out there's not much help. The state doesn't offer much in the way of special benefits for veterans, the school is not going to make any exception for me, thousands of people are competing for work, and a veteran's preference and bachelor's degree doesn't seem to get me picked for work any faster than anyone else. So I'm in a pickle, but the real question is what to tell my son when he gets older.

Am I supposed to tell him that the military will make him feel good about his country? That it will make him feel like he's done something for his community? All I did was piss off a bunch of Iraqis and eat up the tax payers dollars for a war that hasn't done anything for America except make us look like a bunch of bullies. Should I tell my son to get an education and go off to school so he can pursue his interests? What if his interests are in politics too, or worse, philosophy?

Well whatever will be will be and I'm sure I'll get by. I didn't need all that military training and college education to learn how to be a bum. They teach that on TV.

I guess I can thank myself for fighting for the freedom to live off the taxpayer dollar. Unemployment office here I come.

Sun Feb 22, 2009 | 06:30 PM |

After Note: Even though I still do not have a nice high paying job, I do think that the education has been well worth my while. It's the military part that I'm not too sure of, but there are some aspects of my military training that have made me a better person. I tell myself that if I hadn't been to Iraq and seen the violence I did I wouldn't know how awful war is and therefore wouldn't have the strong feeling that I do about violence, war, and U.S. foreign policy in general, but maybe I didn't really need to experience that for that to have happened. I'll never know for sure, and it is what it is, but at least I have the opportunity to express myself freely and exchange ideas with people from all walks of life.

NM Bill Benefits Out of State Residents - No Bill for New Mexico Veterans Though

A bill that would allow residents from outside of New Mexico to be able to pay in state tuition rates is on the governor's desk. Yes, this would bring money from outside of New Mexico, but how does it help veterans who want to go to school already living in New Mexico?

Why aren't our state lawmakers creating ways for New Mexicans (veterans or not) to be able to afford school in New Mexico?

I appreciate the effort to provide more benefits to veterans, but as a New Mexico resident and veteran I find it hard to believe that my lawmakers would approve this bill before coming up with something that will help me and my fellow veterans already paying into the state.

Here's a snippet from the press release:

Santa Fe - On its way to the Governor's desk is Senator Bill Payne's bill to offer in-state tuition at New Mexico universities to honorably discharged veterans, their spouses and children no matter where they live at the same time. The bill sponsored by Senate Minority Whip attracts Federal GI

Bill dollars to New Mexico Universities and to the state's economy. The bill passed the House unanimously minutes ago. It also passed the Senate unanimously. It is estimated that $40 million could pour into the state if 1,000 veterans attend school here.

"This is a way of attracting students to come here who have money from the Federal GI bill for tuition, as well as for living expenses. It is a boon for the state. It is a benefit. Also, it thanks our veterans for their service to our country," Senator Payne said.

Right now, at least 300 veterans would qualify for the program and that could be a $12 million gain for universities and for the economy. "In addition to benefiting the honorably discharged veteran and his or her family, this bill benefits the state of New Mexico and the universities," (BUT NOT NEW MEXICO'S VETERANS) Senator Payne said. "The state would be able to attract veterans to come to New Mexico to study and hopefully make New Mexico their home. The college educated veterans could help improve the state's economic development efforts by attracting more businesses looking for a better educated work-force."

Tue Mar 17, 2009 | 10:17 AM |

House Passes Legislation to Improve Veterans' Benefits, Assist Rural Vets (press release)

Washington, DC – Today, the House of Representatives passed two pieces of legislation cosponsored by Rep. Ben Ray Luján that will help veterans across New Mexico. The Veterans Cost of Living Increase (H.R. 1513) provides a cost of living increase for disability benefits for veterans and dependency and indemnity for their families. The Veterans Emergency Care Reimbursement (H.R. 1377) requires the

Secretary of Veterans Affairs to reimburse veterans receiving emergency treatment in non-Department of Veterans Affairs facilities.

"Rural veterans often are not able to travel to VA facilities for emergency care. The Veterans Emergency Care Reimbursement Act will help them receive emergency care in their communities without traveling long distances to VA facilities," said Rep. Luján. "The Veterans Cost of Living Increase Act will make is easier for veterans who struggle as their cost of living increases without seeing equal increases in their benefits. We have a responsibility to provide our veterans with the benefits they have earned and deserve, and I will continue to fight for veterans throughout New Mexico."
Tue Mar 31, 2009 | 07:28 AM |

Rest in Peace: Joshua M. Carter
Josh was a fellow machine gunner who suffered from PTSD after getting out of the service. He was the type of Marine you always wanted to watch your back. I will never forget him. Josh passed away on March 26, 2009 and is survived by his parents, daughter, brothers, and extended family. A memorial was held for him on April 3, 2009 at Nicholas Catholic Church in North Pole, Alaska.[5]
Wed Apr 1, 2009 | 09:07 PM |

Note: The following post is a poem I wrote while working on this book. I was inspired by news reports of current events and by reading through many of these posts like the one above, which have invoked feelings of disillusionment and confusion. I think this poem reflects those feelings:

Fragmented Thoughts

Conflicted, fragmented, and scattered,
Tragic aftermath, an accident from a nuclear reactor.
It's a disaster. . .
Living life now can be hectic, sometimes it's chaos.
From anarchy to order, hold it all on my shoulders,
Next month it gets colder.
Fill in. . . Fill in. . . Fill in. . .
For words, I'm at a loss. It has to stop.
No balance between the lies & the info ops.
Who are we to blame?
Just sheep & cannon fodder.
Class warfare, but who cares – too apathetic to bother.
Because we have it good. Too good.
The blood stains through,
Why are we all so consumed, with ourselves when the
world's burning down?
Up lift. . . Up lift. . . Up lift. . .
The collective conscious,
Or is it just the NSA's collection of nonsense?
Loyalty doesn't always set the mind free,
But it's done out of necessity. . .
We all live together on this planet,
So why not just get along?
Give it a try before they drop the big bomb.
Mon Dec 10, 2012 | 3:01 PM |

CHAPTER 2 NOTES

[1] Visit http://www.the-independent-newspaper.com.

[2] See Sanger, David E. "Rebel Arms Flow Is Said to Benefit Jihadists in Syria, *The New York Times,* October 14, 2012. http://www.nytimes.com/2012/10/15/world/middleeast/jihadists-receiving-most-arms-sent-to-syrian-rebels.html?hp&pagewanted=all

[3] For more information on New Mexico's medical marijuana program visit the New Mexico Department of Health's Medical Cannabis Program webpage. http://nmhealth.org/idb/medical_cannabis.shtml.

[4] Kaltenback, Emily. Medical Cannabis for Patients with PTSD in New Mexico Is Under Attack, *Huffington Post,* October 16, 2012. http://www.huffingtonpost.com/emily-kaltenbach/medical-cannabis-for-pati_b_1971824.html.

[5] Josh's obituary can be found at the Fairbanks *Daily News-Miner* website at http://www.legacy.com/obituaries/newsminer/obituary.aspx?page=lifestory&pid=125633802#fbLoggedOut.

3| VIOLENT EXTREMISM

DHS Says Returning Vets Potential Recruits For Right Wing Extremists
FROM THE REPORT:
(U) Disgruntled Military Veterans
(U//FOUO) DHS/I&A assesses that rightwing extremists will attempt to recruit and radicalize returning veterans in order to exploit their skills and knowledge derived from
military training and combat. These skills and knowledge have the potential to boost the capabilities of extremists—including lone wolves or small terrorist cells—to carry out
violence. The willingness of a small percentage of military personnel to join extremist groups during the 1990s because they were disgruntled, disillusioned, or suffering from the psychological effects of war is being replicated today.
— (U) After Operation Desert Shield/Storm in 1990-1991, some returning military veterans—including Timothy McVeigh—joined or associated with rightwing extremist groups.

— (U) A prominent civil rights organization reported in 2006 that "large numbers of potentially violent neo-Nazis, skinheads, and other white supremacists are now learning the art of warfare in the [U.S.] armed forces."

— (U//LES) The FBI noted in a 2008 report on the white supremacist movement that some returning military veterans from the wars in Iraq and Afghanistan have joined extremist groups.[1]

MY TAKE:

Everyone bitches and moans that this is unfair and that vets shouldn't be targeted this way, but I'm not surprised at the assessment. Not only are skinheads and neo-Nazis joining the military to learn how to fight, but so are gang members. At least one YouTube video titled "Gang Bangers in the U.S. Military Forces" provides some not so nice details.[2]

But what do you expect? Civil disobedience and crime in many parts of the world can be blamed for the sudden loss of jobs by young males with previous military or police training. When the Soviet Union collapsed and young men in the military, police and intelligence found themselves out of work they turned to what they knew how to do best; kill, intimidate and spy, but they did it for gangs and international criminal networks. The same can be true in other parts of the world like El Salvador, so why would it be any different in the United States?

Unemployment among veterans is higher than the national average, and yes, vets today are trained to kill and many have done so already. Not only are vets trained in warfare, but they have skills in many other areas including communications, small unit leadership, avionics, driving, etc. I completely understand why a returning vet who has above average work skills and has done more than most civilians can become disgruntled when unable to find work. Not to mention the military gives little to no help to many vets who are in need of better health and dental care, educational assistance, housing, etc.

The solution is simple: STOP TREATING ACTIVE DUTY MILITARY MEN AND WOMEN LIKE SHIT AND GIVE THEM THE FINANCIAL ASSISTANCE THEY NEED WHEN THEY GET OUT. We can give officers $60,000 a year pensions, but can't even give an enlisted grunt who served for full four years getting shot at in Iraq proper dental care for a couple months after getting out of the military. BULLSHIT! Well I guess this will put me on the DHS target list, but I've probably been on it for awhile anyway. Luckily for the government I'm not disgruntled, just a bit frustrated with how the whole system works, but I'm trying in the most legal and honest way to make it better.

Fri Apr 17, 2009 | 10:49 AM |

Disconnect

There's a war going on - brought straight to your homes via satellite.
Like video games this war is played. Chess pieces on big screens with gadgets of all types.
Get patriotic, get excited and hyped.
These pieces are people being shifted on the battlefield checkerboard.
And when the blood's drawn the big men tack one off toward their score.
So easily replaceable and forgotten when the pieces withdraw from the game.

Back to the world where the blood only bleeds on the TV
screen.
Wake up in a cold sweat from the nightmares, but no one
hears the screams.
Reality sinks in. No one around understands. Walking around
in this wax museum.
So disconnected. They're disconnected. No connection.
Numb to the world.
There's no pain really, no emotion, no notice. It all seems
hopeless, so why even explain.
It keeps eating at my brain. . .
My brain. . . My brain is washed dirty with rotten thoughts of
death and decay.
Swimming in and slipping in my ways. Take it away.
Take it all, I'll run, I only get closer the harder I try to make
some distance.
Struggle on. Or give in. The battle in the soul can only
withstand so much resistance.
Thu Apr 23, 2009 | 07:41 PM |

After Note: For more poetry check out *Technipoems:
Thoughts on Chaos and War.* Available in print or digital
format at www.lulu.com/spotlight/worldword.

Fort Detrick Bio-Hazhard

The loss of the vials of Venezuelan equine encephalitis
from Fort Detrick has people speculating about the possibility
of a link between the lost vials and the recent outbreak of the
swine flu. The vials were found missing when a researcher
did a full inventory and couldn't account for these vials.
Another researcher said they were probably lost years ago
when a freezer failed and destroyed several samples.

According to the report, the freezer failed before computerized databases were being used. There was no paper record of the freezer failure to verify the researcher's claim.[3]

Venezuelan equine encephalitis is carried by mosquitoes and can cause encephalitis in humans and horses. (21 Horses Die at Palm Beach Polo Match[4] - any connection?) The virus causes flu like symptoms in humans, but rarely causes death. According to emedicine.com the virus "remains a potentially potent biological weapon."[5] The site says the virus "is potentially susceptible to genetic manipulation in advanced laboratories," and that the alpha viruses have "characteristics that make them suited for weaponization." Furthermore, the alpha viruses "could potentially be produced in large quantities and delivered effectively via an aerosol route."

Whether or not there is a direct link to the lost virus and recent swine flu outbreaks doesn't matter. What matters is that these vials of potential biological weapons were not handled properly. Just because there was no computer record of the vials does not mean it is acceptable for them to be unaccounted for. Any kind of computer problem could wipe out the records and thousands more viruses could get lost. A systematic paper record accountability method should be in place at all times. Also, why wasn't the freezer incident recorded? Once again the question of the security of bio-labs comes to light. If military bio-labs in the United States aren't secure enough to know where their materials are, than what can be said about the bio-labs throughout the world which have much less stringent security controls?

Mon Apr 27, 2009 | 06:55 AM |

After Note The security of global bio-labs should be scrutinized severely every day. There should be no reason deadly bio-toxins go unaccounted for in any lab.

Post 9/11 GI Bill Applications Being Taken

As of May 1, 2009 the VA will be accepting applications for the Post 9/11 GI Bill. For those of us who have used up all the entitlements of the Montgomery GI Bill there is still hope. If you qualify, veterans who used all of the MGIB entitlements can still receive up to 12 months of entitlements from the new bill. HOORAH!

For more information on the Post 9/11 GI Bill, visit http://www.gibill.va.gov.

Wed Apr 29, 2009 | 08:16 PM |

NM Guardsman Prepare to Deploy

First published in *The Independent* newspaper.[6]

Estancia - "I heard some of you joking about how I'm going to go over there and kill someone," Capt. Michael Calhoon said. "I hope I don't have to. We're there to help the Iraqi government sustain themselves."

Calhoon, an Estancia Middle School math teacher and National Guardsman about to deploy to Iraq, was talking to the Elementary and Middle School students at the school gym in Estancia on Tuesday, May 5. A special assembly was held for him and Specialist Jordan Brock, an Estancia high school graduate and Guardsman about to deploy to Afghanistan.

Calhoon may not want to have to use lethal force, but he told the students that, "there are people who don't appreciate us being there."

Calhoon had to finish the school year off early so he can take part in pre-deployment training before leaving for

Mosul, Iraq. Calhoon is an infantryman deploying with the 515th Combat Service Support Battalion. He said his duties as a captain have changed and he is not sure exactly what role he will have in the battalion, but he did say he will be working out of forward operating bases' headquarters.

Calhoon will spend 15 months away from family, friends, coworkers and students in a volatile and hostile region, but he is confident in the ability of his command saying, "We are the best trained, best equipped military on the planet."

Although it will be difficult to leave his family, he said it is important for thing at home to be going smoothly.

"Our ability to do the job while deployed has a lot to do with what's going on back home," Calhoon said. "We have to have a clear mind."

Brock, an engineer in the Guard's 920th Engineering Company, said it is important for family and friends to write to the deployed soldiers. The unit, which is slated to help clear roads and minefields, will be on its first combat deployment. Brock will help with building and rebuilding the infrastructure in Afghanistan. He said because he will be back before Calhoon, also his former coach, he will have a dinner arranged upon his return.

The 920th was scheduled to deploy on Monday.

Captain Jason Pete, also a Guardsman, asked students who knew someone who had been deployed, is deployed, or will be deployed. About a quarter of the students in the gym stood up.

He told the students how important of a job the military has in protecting their freedoms, but he also emphasized the importance of everyday heroes like teachers and nurses.

"We leave and fight on foreign soil if necessary to defend our way of life," Pete said. "As soldiers we do what we do because of each one of you here today.

During the assembly students waved American flags and yelled hooahs in support of the soldiers. The high school quartet sang American Tears and the student council presented a gift to Calhoon. A tree will be planted in his honor and a group of students will record everything that goes on at the school while he is gone. Students and teachers will also where red shirts as a respect to the deployed soldiers.

County Commissioner Vanessa Chavez and Estancia Mayor Ted Barela attended the event at which Superintendent Carolyn Allen-Renteria introduced the guests.

"All of us in the crowd support you. We're blessed to have you serving," Renteria said. "We'll miss you."

Wed May 13, 2009 | 07:05 AM |

KAFB Captain to Receive Bronze Star

Capt. Shane Frith, Kirtland Air Force Base airmen, will receive the Bronze Star Medal May 15 at 1 p.m. for his work as an explosive ordinance disposal flight commander during Operation Iraqi Freedom.

Frith led 391 combat missions that destroyed 126 IEDs, he was involved in operations that led to the kill or capture of 6 insurgents and 11 other "high -value" targets.

Frith was responsible for integrating his EOD team with the local Iraqi Police Counter Explosives Team.

The Bronze Star is awarded to any person who distinguishes themselves by heroic or meritorious achievement or service while engaged in military operations involving armed conflict with an enemy.

I don't know Frith, but it sounds like he sure deserves the medal. Anyone willing to risk getting blown up to help provide a safer environment deserves my vote. Hopefully the Iraqi Police he worked with learned something and are successful in reducing the amount of IEDs in Iraq.

It seems like IEDs are the weapon of choice in Iraq and they sure as hell are nasty. Every month someone gets killed by one of these things, and it's usually civilians that get taken out.

Thu May 14, 2009 | 12:56 PM |

Obama Reminds Country of the Meaning of Memorial Day

"That is what Memorial Day is all about. It is about doing all we can to repay the debt we owe to those men and women who have answered our nation's call by fighting under its flag. It is about recognizing that we, as a people, did not get here by accident or good fortune alone. It's about remembering the hard winter of 1776, when our fragile American experiment seemed doomed to fail; and the early battles of 1861 when a union victory was anything but certain; and the summer of 1944, when the fate of a world rested on a perilous landing unlike any ever attempted."

"It's about remembering each and every one of those moments when our survival as a nation came down not simply to the wisdom of our leaders or the resilience of our people, but to the courage and valor of our fighting men and women." - President Barack Obama in his weekly address, Saturday, May 23, 2009 (Text was made available prior to the actual address).[7]

Fri May 22, 2009 | 04:46 PM |

Three Marines Remembered This Memorial Day

I was guarding the gates of Babylon when I heard over the radio that a helicopter had gone down in the nearby river. Soon after a voice came over the radio saying Sgt. Ski was amongst those that had been killed in the accident.

At first I couldn't believe it. What was he doing on the helicopter I asked myself? Something didn't seem right. This wasn't how Sgt. Ski was supposed to go. He was the type that would die jumping on a grenade to save his Marines.

I was soon relieved from my post, but I stayed around the radio waiting to hear more information. I found out later that Ski had not been on the helicopter, but had jumped in the river to try to rescue the downed crew. He ended up getting swallowed in the river as well.

So my intuition was right: Ski died trying to save someone, not by a freak accident.

Sgt. Kirk Allen Straseskie died May 19, 2003 serving his country the only way he knew how. I will always remember Ski as a real hero. Ski's actions that day were unselfish and valiant. Ski will be remembered long past this Memorial Day and the one's to follow. He is in the heart and soul of this country, and lives on in the spirit of democracy and freedom.[8]

I didn't know Sgt. Parkerson had been killed right away because I was already out of the Marines and was going to college. When the word got to me of his death I not only felt sorrow, but I felt guilty as well. Guilty because I wasn't there fighting next to this Marine that had been there for me and the other "boots" he whipped into shape.

Parkerson was a martial arts instructor and taught many of us grappling moves and crowd control maneuvers we often used in Iraq and on each other. Parkerson was the type that would party hard with his younger Marines, but still quick to remind us who was boss.

Sgt. Harvey E. Parkerson III died at age 27 from enemy action in Al Anbar province. I'm sure many beers were poured out in his memory this Memorial Day. Parkerson's fury and good will lives in the battle flags we raise each morning and his fighting spirit flows through the men and women who watch over the land while the rest of us sleep at night.[9]

Carter was the type you wanted to have your back during a firefight in Iraq or in a bar brawl Stateside. Carter was the type of Marine you didn't want to make mad. He had so much piss and vinegar in him you could see it in the sweat on his forehead.

I remember bringing him from Camp Pendleton to Albuquerque while on leave. We partied like there was no tomorrow when we got here. I remember being one of the first people to arrive at a party we found down the street from where we were at. By the time the sun was coming up Carter was clearing out the rooms in traditional Marine Corps urban warfare style. Even on leave he couldn't stop being a hard ass leatherneck.

He slept in the bunk below me on ship, he lived in the room next to me on base, he fought from a couple Amtraks over during the invasion of Iraq and the memories I have of him will rest forever in a special place in my mind.

Joshua M. Carter passed away March 26, 2009 after a long battle with post traumatic stress disorder. Josh was especially with me this Memorial Day.

May all the servicemen and women who passed away in the name of the red, white and blue rest in peace. And may

you forever be remember and honored for the sacrifices you made on behalf of the United States of America.
Sat May 23, 2009 | 06:58 PM |

After Thought: Hopefully the sacrifice is not in vain and the world will one day know peace!

I Need Your Input: What Should A Veterans' Court Consist Of?

Today I attended a veterans' town hall meeting hosted by Rep. Martin Heinrich where veterans were given the opportunity to speak before Heinrich and a panel of state veterans' affairs representatives. Topics addressed included retirement compensation, health care, education benefits and the wars in Iraq and Afghanistan.

I was urged to go before the panel by a member in the audience to speak of the issues I have faced after returning from Iraq. I told the panel that veterans of the most recent conflicts have had it better than the older vets in terms of the services we receive, but I told them I had a couple complaints.

After speaking my mind about vocational rehabilitation entitlements and dental care I asked NM Secretary of Veterans' Affairs John Garcia where the state stood in the creation of a veterans' court. He told me what I already knew: that a committee had been formed to study the possibility of creating such a court. Afterward I was approached by someone from the state veterans' affairs who asked me if I would schedule an appointment with him to discuss my ideas about what a veterans' court should consist of.

I agreed to his proposition and will call next week. I have a few ideas about how such a court should work, but I would like a few suggestions from other veterans. Anyone who reads this please comment about what you think a veterans' court should offer. This is a great opportunity that I will not waste, so please pass this message to any veterans you know so that I can provide more input to the state.

Thanks All, - Scott -

Wed May 27, 2009 | 06:05 PM |

Sandia Labs Veterans Business Meeting (press release)

A town hall meeting for veteran business owners will be held Tuesday, June 16 at the New Mexico Veterans' Memorial at 1 p.m. Sandia National Laboratories' Small Business Utilization Department will explain how veterans can bid on contract with Sandia Labs at the meeting.

According to the U.S. Department of Labor, one out of seven small businesses are veteran owned. In New Mexico there are 22,000 veteran owned small businesses. To find out more about the town hall meeting call (505) 823-2000.

Mon Jun 15, 2009 | 08:53 PM |

Homeless Vets Getting Assistance (press release)

U.S. Secretary of Veterans Affairs Eric K. Shinseki and U.S. Housing and Urban Development Secretary Shaun Donovan announced that $75 million will be used to provide permanent supportive housing and VA case managers for 10,000 homeless veterans.

Approximately 10,000 rental assistance vouchers will be provided to assist homeless veterans across the United States.

"No one, especially veterans who have faithfully served our country should become homeless," Shinseki said.

The housing assistance program will allow veterans to rent privately owned housing. The VA will also provide

eligible homeless veterans health care services. More than
100,000 homeless veterans access VA health care annually.
For more information visit the veteran's affairs supportive
housing program website at
http://www.hud.gov/offices/pih/programs/hcv/vash/.
Sat Jun 20, 2009 | 07:46 AM |

Air Force Space Program Money Passes Armed Services Committee

The National Defense Authorization Act for Fiscal Year 2010[10] passed the U.S. House Armed Service Committee[11] by a vote of 61 to 0 on Wednesday, June 17.

The bill will provide $25 million in funding for Kirtland Air Force Base's Operationally Responsive Space Program. The funding will be used for development and launch costs for the ORS Satellite-1.

The satellite is used for intelligence, surveillance and reconnaissance. In a recent press release it states, "The ability to provide on-demand, multi-spectral images that cover miles of terrain would give our war fighters improved enemy awareness and could ultimately save American lives.

Kirtland Air Force Base's program offers added technology to the national Operationally Responsive Space program.[12]

Sat Jun 20, 2009 | 08:01 AM |

Remembering the Invasion: Camp Commando

We stood twelve hour posts in a tower behind a machinegun in freezing cold temperatures. It really sucked but I will always know how to have patience now. I remember reading a book about the previous U.N. inspectors who had been kicked out while watching new ones traveling toward the Iraqi border while I was on post. When I was relieved I would go to the chow hall and watch CNN show the same U.N. inspectors inside Iraq.

I would always hope to get the post on the Kuwaiti side of the base so I could practice my Arabic, eat some of their chow, and to check out what the Kuwaiti army was all about. During Ramadan they gave me tons of food and tea. They sat around and told stories about the Gulf War.

Several of the Kuwaitis I talked to had fought against the Iraqis right from where I was sitting. One of the Kuwaitis told me he had been held captive by Saddam's army for several years. I heard other stories from the Kuwaitis about the Gulf War. After being overran by the Iraqi military many Kuwaitis were raped and tortured. I was told about relatives who had had their ears and tongues cut off. One Kuwaiti told me about a gunfight at Camp Commando that took the lives of Kuwaitis he served with.

Sometimes we would watch the Kuwaiti Commandos train their recruits. The training included a run around the base where the Kuwaitis would spray the recruits, who were only wearing shorts, with water in the middle of the night while it was freezing cold. We used to watch them do the confidence course where they would climb way up on this tower to climb around on some ropes. The amazing thing was they didn't use any safety equipment at all. The thing that blew my mind about the Kuwaiti's was they didn't seem to have any kind of work schedule. They would arrive in nice sports cars, stand a couple hours of post, and then leave. They told me they not only had free cars and gas, but that they also had free education, were paid tremendously well, and had special privileges like being able to smuggle alcohol across the border without getting in trouble.

Sun Jun 21, 2009 | 09:16 PM |

Death Toll Totals

The Associated Press reported that there were 4,316 U.S. military deaths in Iraq between March 2003 and June 26, 2009. Iraqbodycount.org reports that about 100,000 Iraqi civilians have died from war related violence since the war began. The worst months for Iraqi civilian deaths were in March and April of 2003 at about 7,500 deaths for both months. The same website says one in 160 of Baghdad's 6.5 million people have been violently killed.

Various reports indicate that over 20,000 insurgents have been killed since the war began. Many of the reports vary on the numbers for Iraqi civilians and insurgents killed. Numbers for U.S. deaths do not vary among the different reports.[13]

Fri Jun 26, 2009 | 07:49 PM |

Troops can leave but Iraq cannot be abandoned

From "The Troop Drawdown Could Be Costly for Iraq" (*WSJ*) - *"Power and prestige matter. Withdrawal from Iraq's cities is good politics in Washington, but when premature and done under fire it may very well condemn Iraqis to repeat their past."*[14]

And from the *Washington Post* - *"Obama said Iraq's future was now "in the hands of its own people," and its Sunni, Shi'ite and Kurdish leaders had to make some hard choices to resolve disputes that have been obstacles to real political reconciliation."*

So the question is will the Iraqis be condemned to repeat their past? The violent politics of the past could return to the region once the United States is gone, but unlike in the past the United States now has a duty to do something about it. The U.S. cannot leave Iraq without continuing to provide humanitarian assistance as was the case in Afghanistan after the defeat of the Soviets. Political chaos and violent upheaval can be dealt with by the police and security of local forces, but no one will want to go along the democratic path if the United States is seen as abandoning the people of Iraq.

The United States must continue to provide the necessary resources that will alow the country to have a good education system, modern medicine, access to the media and a strong infrastructure. If the United States does not provide aide and guidance to strengthen the fragile democratic institutions within Iraq then we may very well see the Iraqi people be condemned to repeat their past, just as the United States will be condemned to repeat the past mistakes that were made in Afghanistan and so many other countries the U.S. has used military force in.

The military did its job which was to fight the Baathists and the insurgents, and now the forces must leave to allow local security to take over and for the people to police themselves. Rebuilding Iraq into a democratic nation is not the job of the military, as the military is the United States' least democratic institution. Now it is time for real democracy to take shape in the country which will occur as long as the Iraqi people can be shown that democracy does not abandon the people it tries to convert.

And if the country does return to a violent authoritarian regime where political violence is the only way to power, then the United States must not return with their guns blazing. Instead, the United States must rally support from the international community to take action, rather than doing it alone. The unilateral approach the U.S. took on Iraq before the invasion only destroyed the legitimacy of the United States' claim to democracy while also tearing apart the foundations of the United Nations which the U.S. worked so hard to build.

Tue Jun 30, 2009 | 12:08 PM |

Anxiety

Fireworks cause anxiety among combat vets. The best solution? Go somewhere more peaceful until the Fourth of July is over.

Tue Jun 30, 2009 | 12:24 PM |

After Note: While working on this book a neighbor living one street over decided to blow up a bunch of fireworks in the middle of a normal December day. I was talking to a friend who has no combat experience at the time, but when the fireworks started going off we both thought we were being shelled. After ducking our heads and being paranoid for a bit we realized it was just fireworks, but the funny (or not-so-funny) thing is that we were not the only ones who thought a war was going on outside. My wife soon emerged from the house wanting to know what was going on, as did just about everyone else on the block who were all looking a little nervous. So really it's not that strange for people to be anxious and paranoid over fireworks. It happens to vets and non-vets alike. The sad thing is if we were really being attacked all of us were doing the wrong thing by exposing ourselves on the street. But hey, curiosity can get the best of us all sometimes.

There are tons of triggers for vets, but fireworks may be one of the worse, however Halloween can be pretty nerve wracking as well. . .

Biden to Discuss Long-Term Stability with Iraqi Leaders

According to a White House press release, U.S. Vice President Joe Biden is in Iraq to visit with troops and to discuss the troop drawdown with Iraqi leaders.

The press release says, "He will discuss with Iraq's leaders the importance of achieving the political progress that is necessary to ensure the nation's long-term stability."[15]

I hope he is discussing what type of educational, medical, and infrastructure assistance the United States will provide to ensure this long-term stability, because without this assistance the U.S. will surely fail in creating a stable long-term ally in Iraq.

The U.S. military can proudly walk away as victors in Iraq, having accomplished the mission of destroying any means the country had to build WMDs, while also overthrowing Saddam Hussein and creating a new semi-democracy that is friendly to the U.S., however the *American people* cannot claim victory until 20 or 30 years from now when we know that the country has gained the long-term stability Biden is discussing.

Once we have seen that the country has become an active and engaged world player which seeks to cooperate with the countries surrounding it and the rest of the international community than the United States its people can claim victory. For this is what is in the U.S.' best interests and this is, or should be, the true goal of the U.S.' war in Iraq.

Now that the troops will be coming home, the U.S. can engage in a true democratic form of nation building, using the diplomatic corps to bring fresh innovative ideas to the country in order to create a long lasting friendship between the two nations.

Fri Jul 3, 2009 | 05:25 PM |

Magnetic Bombs and the Future of Warfare
From "Round-up of Daily Violence in Iraq" - Sunday 5 July, 2009 (McClatchy):
"Diyala - A magnetic bomb was stuck to a civilian car and detonated at 11.30 a.m. Sunday in al Mualimeen neighbourhood. The explosion killed the driver and injured two civilian passers by."[16]

Wow, this sure makes it easy to blow stuff up. Just slap this bomb on anything metal and walk away. It seems like criminals are becoming more innovative every day. The more technologically advanced their opposition is the more creative they become. It just goes to show that if an insurgent has his mind set on killing someone than he will kill someone, no matter who it is. It's like they want to cause chaos just for the sake of causing chaos.

I'm not sure I quite understand why an insurgent would slap a magnetic bomb on any random vehicle, but I guess they think it will benefit their cause. The longer I've been out of the Marines the more strange I find all this violence to be.

It seems to me like these insurgents are not just going to go away. They have managed to stay active throughout the U.S. military campaign in Iraq and have been able to spread their ideals throughout the globe. It will be impossible to capture or kill all the terrorists in the world, so what I suggest is a new strategy:

The military should cross-train soldiers in police-type work to include swat tactics, detective work and undercover operations in order to combat terrorists worldwide. The military should create more small special operations type units and spread them throughout the globe on sea, in the air, and on the ground to combat international criminal networks like al Qaeda who continue to move from place to place without regard to borders.

It does not make sense to pile all of America's troops into one country to fight an enemy that is not restricted by borders. With smaller military units positioned around the globe the U.S. can track, kill, capture or deter more terrorists in more places. The U.S. should go at it alone and covertly in places that do not wish to cooperate, and overtly with others in places that do.

At first glance this may seem like I am proposing a world police state with the U.S. leading the way in providing the security apparatus, however this is exactly the opposite of what I am proposing. A world police state will occur if we let the war on terrorism evolve on its own. If the U.S. continues to fight this war as it has been doing than what we will see is a continuation of large scale military operations in different countries, by not just the U.S, but Russia, China and India as well. Each excursion will leave behind a militarized state with an organized police force prepared to fight alongside the larger nation which has propped it up. This is what happened during the Cold War and what is continuing to happen now.

What I propose will create a de-militarization of nations by using small, unseen forces to do the dirty work, while the larger forces remain out of the limelight. By spreading these smaller units throughout the globe the U.S. can collect better intelligence while also building stronger relations with countries that would otherwise go unnoticed in Washington. It is important to focus on the deterrence factor that can be brought with such a restructuring of the military. Not only can these smaller units move in and out of countries unnoticed and conduct better cross-national training exercises, but they can also bring in much needed assistance to the countries they will be deployed in or near.

Many of these units will have plenty of down time to build better relations by providing humanitarian assistance to people in need. By providing this assistance the U.S. can prevent impoverished people from wandering into a life of crime. The military has the tools to provide this type of assistance, but without a strong civilian corps to do the work it may be impossible to bring assistance everywhere it is needed.

The more civilians that can be used to bring in medical supplies, books, food and infrastructure tools, the less the military will be needed in these areas and could eventually be phased out or used only as a small observatory security force, depending on how active international criminals continue to be in these countries.

The war on terrorism really is a police action that should be fought as such, but at the same time the military should be prepared for conventional warfare as well. If an enemy wants to fight in a designated area using traditional military frontline fighting tactics where uniforms and insignia are still worn than the U.S. should be ready for that, but they should be prepared for global police work as well, which the U.S. is not.

Yes, the U.S. military has become more accustomed to fighting a guerilla type war, but they have not beaten the enemy at their own game. The enemy knows that the U.S. will stop short of sending troops into Somalia or Yemen, which is why they are fleeing there. They know they can blend in as civilians in Europe and North America without the fear of having a battalion of Marines sent after them.

The U.S. needs to be three or four steps ahead of al Qaeda and other terrorist networks, but so far they are not. As long as the U.S. military continues to send more troops into Afghanistan while ignoring other terrorists' safe havens across the globe they will always remain a few steps behind. It is time to restructure our military, not as a reaction to terrorists, but as an offensive move to prepare for the future of warfare.

Now if only we can figure out how to prevent warfare in the first place. . .

Sun Jul 5, 2009 | 08:34 PM |

Remembering the Invasion: Psyops, Rockets & Confusion
First published in *The Independent* newspaper.[17]

The psychological operations taking place in Afghanistan today are much different than the psyops we used during the 2003 invasion of Iraq. Often times we would use loudspeakers to announce our presence to the Iraqis. Although I couldn't understand the Arabic that was blaring from the speakers, I was told that we were trying to coax the fedayeen into fighting us by insulting their manhood. It was explained that this would bring them out of their hiding spots to separate them from the civilians they would position themselves next to. On at least one occasion the psyops had an adverse effect on me. . .

We had taken over some fighting positions that a previous unit was holding before we got there. We were still moving up the main highway on our way toward Baghdad, about two or three weeks into the invasion, and the fog of war had started to take its toll on me.

The unit before us had shot a vehicle the previous night and it was just sitting in the middle of the road all burned up. As soon as we got to our new position my machinegun team moved to a berm and dug out a good hole where we camouflaged the gun. We were in a pretty good fighting hole, but we weren't being very aggressive. People were walking past us all day checking out our positions. I wanted to go out in front of the berm to question them but I was also scared of land mines.

When night fell I stayed up trying to be as attentive as possible. I was on post staring through the night vision when it was about time to wake up my ammo man, Bonillia. I noticed that there were lights beaming at me from all directions. I thought there were vehicles all around us.

"Wake up," I told Bonilla.

He did quickly and I briefed him on the situation. I wasn't sure what the lights were or who they belonged to, but, despite my apprehension, I still wanted to lie down to get some rest. As soon as I bunkered down for the night bright flashes of light burst in the air.

"Get down!" I said, "Don't let them see you."

I thought we were surrounded and under attack. More flares went off and then I heard Arabic blaring out from somewhere behind me. I thought the fedayeen were screaming at us and were about to assault us from all sides.

"Stay low," I told Bonillia, and then attempted to wake my team leader. He continued to sleep however so we made do without him.

"Do you see anything?" I asked.

"No. I don't see nothing," Bonillia said.

"Incoming rocket!" someone yelled.

"Get down! Get down!" I told Bonilla.

We popped our heads back up and stared out into the darkness as more rockets came our way. A couple impacted directly behind us where Weapons Company was posted. I scanned the entire area with my night vision goggles on, but I couldn't see anything. Machinegun bursts were coming from our right flank shooting tracers in the direction my gun was pointed. I kept looking through the night vision scope on our gun but still didn't see anything. The team to our right unloaded about a thousand rounds into what appeared to be an empty field.

Eventually the shooting ended and the rockets subsided and I managed to get about an hour of sleep before being woken up to stand post again. In the morning we were debriefed and told that two Iraqis had been killed and that the flares were ours all along and the blaring Arabic was coming from the loudspeakers mounted on one of our vehicles. If the speakers were being used to draw enemy fire than I guess it worked, but the psychological impact it had on me was probably not what our commanders were thinking of when they ordered the loudspeakers to be played.

Thu Jul 9, 2009 | 04:52 AM |

My Dad's War: Going back to Vietnam

The following is a letter my father wrote to a friend after returning home from a trip to Vietnam where he was visiting my brother in Hanoi. The last time my dad was in Vietnam was some forty-two years ago when he was sent there as a Marine to fight the VC.

Vietnam: 42 Years Later

By Rick Albright

The Vietnam war has never left me. It is always in the back of my mind, waiting for the slightest suggestion to remind me it is there. I feel a deep sense of loss for the men who died in the war. Although I did not slog through the mud taking small arms fire on a daily basis, I justified the killing of our enemies and accepted collateral damage as an unavoidable part of war. The war didn't stop when I got back to the states. It seemed as if the protestors were yelling at me making me feel as if it had been wrong to serve my country. It was on the TV news every night, until finally I watched as all the places I had defended began to fall to the North Vietnamese army. The South Vietnamese army, we had trained and supplied, melted away as the enemy marched south. First it was Con Thien, then Quang Tri, followed by Dong Ha, Hue, Danang and in 1975 the government we had shed our blood for surrendered. It was a numbing experience for me. After eighteen months in Vietnam I had returned to the United States a skeptic of my government's intentions and disappointed in military life, but I never imagined the North Vietnamese would defeat us.

Over the years I had some opportunities to visit Vietnam as a tourist, but always rejected them. I was reluctant to deal with my emotions which were primarily a deep sense of sadness whenever I thought about Vietnam. In 2011 my oldest son and his family moved to Vietnam. Jeremy and his wife Janet went to work for an International school in Hanoi. The enemy's capital. I knew that I had to visit them from the moment they said they were going. It was the motivation I needed to kick some ghosts out of my life. In the summer of 2012 I returned to Vietnam and was surprised by my feelings.

The sense of guilt was the ghost I wanted to kick out. Not for what I had done, but what I had been willing to do. I felt guilty that I had been a willing dupe of my government and had reveled in the sense of becoming a warrior who would willingly kill others to further a government mission I didn't understand. I also felt guilty about being alive and somewhat unscathed when so many of my peers were dead, wounded in body and soul. What the trip to Vietnam did was help me come to some kind of agreement with myself that the guilt is forgivable.

What surprised me the most was the conflicting depth of my pride as a Marine in the job we had done as warriors. I thought all remnants of boot camp had been purged from my soul over the years, but in Saigon (I cannot call it Ho Chi Minh City) I met with a situation I hadn't anticipated. As I peered through the stately fence encompasing the unification palace my mind recalled that last time I had seen this elegant government building surrounded by lush yards and gardens was on TV. This was where the president of South Vietnam lived and ran government during the war. In 1975 all of America watched our allies beg and plead for us to take them away before the North Vietnamese Army entered the palace grounds and the South Vietnamese government surrendered. It is a horrible memory for all Americans who saw it. The people whose freedom we had died for were fleeing from the people we had fought to keep them free. The images in my mind were of people climbing over the fence, helicopters ferrying people to our ships, and scared souls hanging on to the struts of the helicopters as they took off. It was an emotional and embarrassing moment for our country and for me personally.

As I was remembering why I knew this place, a group of men caught my attention. They were for a gathering for a picture. They were shaking hands, and high fiving each other. While I watched, the photographer gathered them into a group so that he could capture this important time in their lives. They were smiling as they put their arms around each other's shoulders and froze for that moment so the camera could archive this image for them. They were war veterans just like me, they were my age, they had survived a war just like me. But, they were veterans who had wanted to kill me and whom I wished to kill. It suddenly struck me that they had won and my heart was full of anger. All of the death, all of the training, all of money, all of the battles we won, all of the pride my country and I had brought to this land meant nothing. These guys, standing right in front of me, had, in the end, defeated us. It made me mad and I felt the footprint of their boot on my ass. I rediscovered that Marines do not take defeat lightly, it makes them cry.

I had to walk away and could not visit the palace until the next day after I had calmed down. That visit brought me some solace. The displays of their victory in the museums of the palace made me realize I was in a place for them. Their people had united and defeated an invader and replaced a corrupt dictatorship that was oppressing their people. The message to me was the same as our message to the Japanese who visit Pearl Harbor. Don't do this again! Their displays were biased and political causing me to understand that the government leaders, like their counterparts in Washington DC, were attempting to build national pride. I was able to view the situation a little more objectively in this context. I had never hated the Vietnamese people, it was the war we fought that I hated.

Walking around Saigon made me realize that in some ways all of us won. Capitalism is alive and well in the largest city in Vietnam and I felt a sense of freedom from oppression as I walked through the streets. Burger King (Macdonald's is working on it) is on the corner, the ports on the river are bustling and the many skyscrapers that have risen since the war attest to the financial growth of Vietnam. They, like the Chinese are using the engine of capitalism to create 21st century infrastructure for their countries. International banks, insurance companies and all the types of business one would see in New York are on display in Saigon. I think that Ho Chi Minh might be rolling in his mausoleum! Maybe that is the footprint on his ass!

After a couple days in Saigon we went to Danang. I had been stationed there during part of my tour and it felt familiar but different. What was happening in Saigon was happening on a smaller scale in that town on a beach of the China Sea. The city is growing and developing into a modern metropolis. It had the feel of a California beach town fifty years ago.

We stayed at a hotel on China Beach and my grandkids had a great time in the water. It was as hot as I remembered but the people were much friendlier and I was having more fun that the last time I was there. People would smile at us, say hello and were interested in our stories. One evening sitting at a table outside of our hotel, my son and I were drinking beer with a couple young of men close to Jeremy's age. Both of my grandsons were sitting with us drinking cokes. One of Vietnamese men looked at me and asked, "Is this your first time here?"

What a loaded question, many thoughts rolled through my mind and I wondered a bit how to answer. I decided to be candid and I said, "No, I was here in 1969, as a Marine, during the war. I lived right up the street at Camp Horne."

He smiled at me, took a drink of his beer and said, "My father was VC then."

I hesitated remembering the lone mortar man so many years ago on the road from Con Thien. This guy's Dad could have been the man. I replied, "Oh, so he was the one who fired a mortar at me? He missed me you know"

We all smiled at each and then we all chuckled and raised our glasses in a toast. How happy I was that his father and I had both survived.   The war is over. For me.

Reading Note: More of Rick's writing can be found online at storymist.com. His book, *Bomb's Away Buckaroos!! The Diaries of a WWII B-24 Crew,* can be purchased at lulu.com/spotlight/rickalbright, or scan the code on pg. 63.

CHAPTER 3 NOTES

[1] The original DHS report was apparently leaked to the media. The report can be found via the Federation of American Scientists. See U.S. Department of Homeland Security. Rightwing Extremisim Current Economic and Political Climate Fueling Resurgence in Radicalization and Recruitment, April 7, 2009. http://www.fas.org/irp/eprint/rightwing.pdf.

[2] Gang Bangers in U.S. Military Forces, YouTube. Uploaded by mav333 on June 29, 2006. http://www.youtube.com/watch?v=1gqShQTSDCM. For an even more in-depth video see Gangland – Basic Training, YouTube. Uploaded by kecho619, January 11, 2012. http://www.youtube.com/watch?v=y7YOW2h0umw.

[3] The *Washington Post* did reported in a separate article that some 9,000 vials of dangerous toxins had been unaccounted for prior to an inventory that was conducted after it was discovered that there were inconsistincies in the actual amount of Venezuelan equine encephalitis virus vials there were and the amount listed in the database. See Hernandez, Nelson. "Fort Detrick Inventory Turns Up 9,220 More Vials of Pathogens, June 18, 2009. http://www.washingtonpost.com/wp-dyn/content/article/2009/06/17/AR2009061703271.html.

[4] Michels, Scott and Sharyn Alfonsi. "21 Horses Die Suddenly at Palm Beach Polo Match," *ABC News,* April 20, 2009. http://abcnews.go.com/Health/story?id=7380774&page=1#.ULZ95IdTySo.

[5] Werlet, Robert W. CBRNE – Venezuelan Equine Encephalitis, *Medscape Reference.* http://emedicine.medscape.com/article/830478-overview

[6] Albright, Scott. "Estancia honors soldiers as they get ready to go to war," *The Independent,* May13-19, 2009, p. 3.

[7] For the full text of the weekly address see http://www.whitehouse.gov/the-press-office/embargoed-weekly-address-president-obama-calls-all-americans-honor-service-troops-a.

[8] To read Sgt. Straseskie's obituary visit http://www.legacy.com/obituaries/washingtonpost/obituary.aspx?n=kirk-allen-straseskie&pid=3097184#fbLoggedOut.

[9] To read Sgt. Parkerson's obituary in the *Los Angeles Times* visit http://articles.latimes.com/2004/aug/29/local/me-parkerson29.

[10] OpenCongress. "H.R. 2647 – National Defense Authorization Act for Fiscal Year 2010." http://www.opencongress.org/bill/111-h2647/text..
[11] http://armedservices.house.gov/
[12] For more information on the Operationally Responsive Space program visit http://ors.csd.disa.mil/index.html.
[13] For an example of official government reports see Fischer, Hannah, "Iraq Casualties U.S. Military Forces and Iraqi Civilians, Police, and Security Forces," Congressional Research Service, June 11, 2010. http://fpc.state.gov/documents/organization/145113.pdf AND U.S. Department of Defense, "U.S. Casualty Status Fatalaties as of November 28, 2012. http://www.defense.gov/news/casualty.pdf.
[14] Rubin, Michael. "Troop Drawdown Could Be Costly For Iraq," *The Wall Street Journal*, June 30, 2009. http://online.wsj.com/article/SB124631741892070801.html.
[15] The White House, Office of the Vice President. "Vice President Biden in Iraq to Meet with Iraqi Leaders and Visit U.S. Troops," July 2, 2009. http://www.whitehouse.gov/the-press-office/vice-president-biden-iraq-meet-with-iraqi-leaders-and-visit-us-troops.
[16] Issa, Sahar. "Round-up of Daily Violence in Iraq – Sunday 5 July, 2009," *McClatchy Newspapers,* July 5, 2009. http://www.mcclatchydc.com/2009/07/05/71271/round-up-of-daily-violence-in.html.
[17] Albright, Scott. "When psyops were different," *The Independent,* July 8, 2009.

Bombs Away Buckaroos!!
Diaries of a WWII B-24 Crew
By Rick Albright

4| INFO OPS & UNEMPLOYMENT

Moriarty Soldier Spreads Radio News to Afghans
First published in *The Independent* newspaper.[1]

Just as thousands of recently deployed Marines began their new mission in Helmand province, Afghanistan, fresh violence sparked off in the eastern Paktika province, near the Pakistan Afghanistan border, which claimed the lives of two U.S. soldiers on Saturday.[2] According to one media report, insurgents used small arms, rockets, mortar rounds, an explosive-filled truck and at least one shell filled with white phosphorous during an attack at a small base in the Zerok district of the province.[3] This came just days after another soldier went missing in the same region and is believed to be held captive by Taliban forces.

The *Los Angeles Times* reported that the capture of the soldier could provide the Taliban with a "propaganda bonanza," which is exactly what one local New Mexican soldier has been trying to prevent from happening in the country.[4]

Moriarty High School graduate Thomas Castillo is currently in Paktia province, just north of Paktika, where he helps to broadcast news radio to the remote parts of the country in an effort to prevent the Taliban from spreading their own version of the news. A recent *Stars and Stripes* article explains how Castillo's unit hands out crank-powered radios in remote villages so the U.S. can be the first to deliver the news before the Taliban has a chance to add their own twist to it.[5] Whenever an incident occurs, like the kidnapping of 16 Afghan de-miners in Paktia on Sunday, Castillo's unit writes a radio story and sends it to disc jockeys that broadcast the event in the local language.[6] The head of the district where the incident occurs is also contacted to ask for advice on how to handle the situation.

Castillo's role is to work on computers and set up transmitters to ensure the broadcasts will be delivered. The idea behind the mission is to build support among the population by broadcasting information about what the Army is doing to assist civilians. The Army will inform radio listeners as to where a mortar attack is occurring so they can seek safety, or will explain how the U.S. is providing humanitarian assistance in the area. Without the Army broadcasts locals will be subjugated to Taliban propaganda which is often inaccurate and potentially harmful for U.S. Afghan relations.

"The Taliban put up a lot of propaganda," Castillo's father, Mike Hoitt, said during a phone interview last week. "They might say America is doing this to you or America is doing that. Now they [U.S. Army] have their own radios so they can report the truth."

Castillo's mother, Tracy Hoitt, said her son has seen some positive signs the mission is working. "He said they're thrilled. They like the interaction with the Americans and that they're really happy to get the radios because they're [Taliban] attacking their people just as much as we're trying to protect them," Tracy Hoitt said. "The radios help them to know the truth about what's happening."

Castillo's grandmother, Terry Myrick, also thinks the Army is making a difference. She said the radio broadcasts are beneficial, "Because that helps people over there like us and work with us.""You know you couldn't breathe without getting in trouble out there," Myrick continued. "Now we're actually helping the people. They give food to them and go to remote villages and help people. All that the Taliban does is cause trouble and bomb people that don't deserve to be bombed. They bomb their own people."

Myrick said Castillo cannot discuss everything he does because of the classified nature of his work, but he does talk about everyday things and asks for more Ramen noodles whenever he does get the chance to call back home. Myrick said nobody wants to see a family member sent off to war, but even so, she is proud of what her grandson is doing.

"In a year he's become a man," she said. "When he was here this kid was going nowhere. Every time I hear something from him I'm just so proud of him." Myrick said Castillo was the type of kid that had difficulty in school and after graduation didn't have much going for him except a job at the Connection.

According to Myrick, Castillo realized he was going nowhere and wanted to do something about it, which is why he joined the Army. "You don't have to stay stagnate all your life," Myrick said. "There's more than Moriarty. There's more in the world."

Castillo's parents weren't ecstatic about their son going off to war, but both seem proud of what he is doing and both are getting the support from the community to make the stress of the situation a bit easier. "Small communities do better than the larger ones," Mike Hoitt said, adding that friends and neighbors are always asking if they need anything for care packages.

For information on sending a care package to deployed soldiers contact the Rio Grande Valley Chapter Blue Star Mothers by visiting nmrgvbluestarmothers.org.

"My biggest thing is whether you're for it or against it, support your soldiers because they don't have a choice," Mike Hoitt said.

Thu Jul 9, 2009 | 04:58 AM |

What N.M.'s Veteran Court Should Be Like

Thousands of veterans returning from Iraq and Afghanistan have begun to return to life as civilians in New Mexico, but many of them may not have an easy time adjusting to their new environment. Some veterans will disregard the laws of the state and may find themselves in front of a judge or in jail. Any new veterans' court the state creates must be designed to help these veterans get back on track, rather than focusing on punishing them for their misdeeds. It is understood that the state will not refer violent criminals to the veterans' court, although I propose that some violent cases, including some domestic violence and assault cases involving self defense, be tried in a veterans' court. The most important thing to remember when trying to help troubled vets is that fear cannot be used to force them into compliance. These men and women were trained to be fearless in battle and faced death on a daily basis while serving overseas. The state must not try to coerce veterans into compliance through the fear of going to jail. A veteran who has served in combat will not fear the use of force by police, nor will they fear spending a few months in jail, as the allowable amount of force police can use on a suspect is nowhere near as scary as what the enemy is allowed to do in Iraq and Afghanistan, and jail is more like a vacation than punishment when compared to being in a combat zone.

What I propose is that the state use a carrot and stick approach when dealing with veterans who have broken the law. Law enforcement officials should immediately determine whether the suspect they have apprehended is a veteran (even better if they can do this beforehand) in order to determine the proper action that must be taken. Law enforcement should be trained in how to deal with combat veterans in order to prevent the escalation of force that is bound to occur when confronting a veteran who is faced with a fight or flight decision. If police know they are dealing with a combat vet than they should use every means possible to deescalate the situation, rather than resorting to violent force. Vets that are booked and processed into a holding facility should immediately be evaluated for mental health disorders including post-traumatic stress disorder, traumatic brain injury, depression, and anger. A Veterans Affairs administrator should provide the evaluation at the holding facility as soon as possible.

Veterans who are determined to have a disorder related to their combat experience should be removed from general population and placed in a rehabilitation/recovery facility or on house arrest before further action is taken. While awaiting a hearing before a judge these veterans should be given proper access to treatment at the VA or through other providers free of charge. It should be determined what type of care should be given on a case-by-case basis. Veterans should be provided with free representation and should be allowed to explain to a judge why their experience in the military has created difficulties as a civilian. Each judge should determine what type of program the veteran will go into at this point. If the judge decides that a veteran is in need of further counseling and other medical treatment than the vet should be allowed to continue to go to the VA hospital, the Vet Center, or other veteran outreach centers to receive treatment. If it is determined that a veteran must be placed on an extended period of house arrest or do jail time, than veteran services should be provided to the veteran at a location they can easily access, which may include medical treatment, benefits assistance, help finding a job or getting into school and financial and housing assistance. Veterans who have problems with alcohol and drugs should be tested frequently for use, but should not be thrown out of the program or placed back in jail for a first time failure. It would be more beneficial to increase counseling services.

Many veterans have had success in recovery by attending programs where they leave the state to participate in a program specifically for veterans on a ranch or camp-like environment. Those who are successful in their program should be rewarded with the opportunity of completing their sentence earlier. If a veteran is placed on house arrest for six months and has met all the requirements of the program for the first two months than the state should consider decreasing the amount of time spent on house arrest. A veteran that goes above and beyond the requirements (i.e. does voluntary work on top of community service) should be the first to be considered for a decreased sentence. And the opposite should occur for those that fail in the program. More time in the program should be added on to those that do not meet the requirements and these veterans should not receive benefits assistance, financial guidance or job placement until they have proven to meet the requirements of the program, such as having clean alcohol and drug tests, completing weekly community service projects and or providing reparations to the victims of their crimes.

For homeless veterans I propose a program similar to Habitat for Humanity where they are given housing vouchers for completion of a community service program involving housing development. These veterans will be taught a job skill that will last them a lifetime, such as carpentry, tiling, roofing, etc., while also giving them a place to live. Veterans who receive a voucher and who complete whatever is required of them by the court should have access to social workers for the rest of their lives if they need it to help them stay off the streets.

The veterans' court should not be designed in a similar fashion as the DWI/Drug Court. The issues veterans face are completely different than what other civilians face and should be treated as such. The DWI/Drug Court program may be successful in preventing future drug use and DWIs, but it will not work to help treat post traumatic stress disorder, traumatic brain injury, and other military related problems. The veterans' court should not be more painful than jail or whatever sentencing they would receive if they were not a veteran. If a veteran realizes that it will be quicker and easier to go to jail then to go through a veterans' program than they will choose jail and the problems will not be fixed. Veterans who violate the law must be held accountable for their actions and should have to repay the victims and the communities for their crimes, but they should not be treated as though they have not already served their country. For those who have served in places like Vietnam, Iraq, and Afghanistan it is difficult to understand why it is not okay to do one thing when they had previously been allowed to do things that were much worse according to local laws.

Thu Jul 9, 2009 | 05:03 AM |

After Note: New Mexico is now home to a veteran's court, something I continue to believe is a much needed service for the state and the country. The court began inductions in November 2011.[7] According to the State of New Mexico Second Judicial District Court website, one must meet the following criteria to be considered for the Veterans Court program: have served in the U.S. military, have an Axis I diagnosis including co-occurring disorders such as Trauma Spectrum Disorder and substance abuse disorder, be competent to stand trial, voluntarily participate in the program, comply with supervision mandates and directives of the assigned Veterans Court supervising officer, adhere to prescribed treatment program, submit to random drug and alcohol screening, and comply with the Veterans Court Agreement. For more information about applicable charges, the court's history, and the court's Peer Mentor Program visit www.veteranscourt2.net.

Jakarta Bomb Blast to the Past

Today, July 17, two bombs went off in two separate hotels in Jakarta, Indonesia, killing eight and injuring dozens more.[8] The group thought to be responsible for the attack is an al-Qaeda branch of Jemaah Islamiyah.

While living in Jakarta in the early 90's I never thought about terrorism and had no fear of being a potential target for a group like Jemaah Islamiyah. I was old enough to know about crime and terrorism and understood that it was a dangerous world, but Islamic extremism didn't seem like much of a threat even though I was living in the most populous Muslim country in the world. In fact, I enjoyed learning about Islam and would visit mosques, talk with Muslims about the religion and even join in during festivities around Idul Fitri. I found most Indonesians to be pleasant and easy enough to get along with, but I did face some hostilities on the streets and was aware of the mob mentality that would take over during large events like the Metallica concert where Indonesians looted and destroyed businesses after too many tickets were sold.

Of course I always thought most of the hostility Indonesians felt towards foreigners was directed at the Chinese, but I did occasionally get harassed for being American. It's hard to imagine that today there are violent extremists throughout the island nation that seek to kill people like me.

What I remember of Indonesia is that I was free to do as I pleased as a foreigner, and was generally treated with kindness by the locals. I remember the tropical beauty of Pulau Seribu and Bali, the Burubudur on Java, and the excitement and thrill of the big city in Jakarta. Now that I'm older and have seen the violence Indonesians are capable of I have a different mentality about what the country really is. Perhaps it's not as safe a place for Americans as I thought it was, and perhaps it is not a place I want to return to as an adult.

It's sad that because of these violent extremists people like myself have to think twice about visiting the country which offers so much diversity in its culture and so much beauty in its landscape.

Fri Jul 17, 2009 | 07:58 AM |

Psychological-Cyber Warfare

From "U.S. condemns video of missing soldier" (South Asia Reuters): *"KABUL - The U.S. military on Sunday denounced the release of a video showing a soldier captured in Afghanistan, saying the images were Taliban propaganda that violated international law."[9]*

I tried tracking down the Taliban video on Google and YouTube, but was unable to find it. With the military denouncing it and calling it illegal propaganda we must wonder if the U.S. government hasn't purposely made the hostage video inaccessible as part of their efforts to engage in psycho-cyber warfare.

Psychological warfare has become an integral part of fighting al Qaeda and the Taliban and the hostage video shows that the Taliban are fully aware of the ability to influence the war through anti-American propaganda. The repercussions of the psychological war have yet to be fully examined.

Americans have become fearful and reactionary to domestic media blitzes and foreign propaganda alike. The hands spinning the wheels behind the media machine aren't always easy to follow and I regret to say it makes me doubtful of the sincerity of all who attempt to control human behavior through psychological warfare.

There are those who engage in it unknowingly and there are those who control the main puppet strings, and it is the latter we should be trying to understand so we can determine which direction we are being led. The continuation of psychological warfare in the war on terror will undoubtedly affect world politics and will ultimately be the deciding factor in how a victory is claimed by either side.

Sooner or later Americans are going to be tired of having their troops deployed to combat zones all the time and the media will reflect the sentiment, and political decisions will be made based on calls from the public to end the war. In the meantime al Qaeda and the Taliban will have continued to operate in locations outside of Afghanistan. If Americans exit Afghanistan while al Qaeda continues to operate in multiple countries the United States cannot claim victory.

The borderless war has made it impossible for the U.S. to eradicate Islamic extremism worldwide and the number of extremists will grow if the U.S. kills civilians and if allegations of wrongdoings by the U.S. government continue.

Perhaps the only way to win the war with Islamic extremism is through psychological war. To beat al Qaeda the U.S. must convince the rest of the world that jihad is the wrong answer and U.S. policies will benefit the whole world. If enough people are convinced of this the jihadists will be minimized to no more than a soft threat. The most important thing for the U.S. to do will be to prove the ideas and policies of America are not only better than jihadist ideas, but it must also behave ethically while engaging the enemy.

What I propose is that the U.S. intensify the war effort in Afghanistan while preparing to pull out completely to reassess the global security threats the U.S. faces from other locations in the world. A quick change of the U.S. military formation will throw al Qaeda off guard, especially after being hit hard in Afghanistan. At the same time the U.S. should engage more efforts in the psycho-cyber war in order to reach more people tempted by jihad. Al Qaeda will not be able to keep up with the information flow and will, in a generational period of time, slowly decrease in numbers.

A new stance on the war on terror should not be a military effort alone. Intelligence agencies, the State Department, US AID, civil service organizations, NGOs and the general public should all synchronize their efforts in spreading American ideologies to the rest of the world. We should fill the airwaves and cyber world with information that encourages peace, cooperation, respect, and generosity in order to prevent minds from being swayed by violent ideologies. The key however is to be able to talk the talk and walk the walk at the same time.

Sat Jul 18, 2009 | 09:04 PM |

After Note: From the mouth of Lenin:

"Freedom of the press is freedom for the political organizations of the bourgeoisie. To give these people such a weapons as the press is to help our enemy. . . In the capitalist world, freedom of the press represents the freedom to buy the newspapers and those who edit them, as well as the freedom to buy, corrupt and mould public opinion in the interests of the bourgeoisie."[10]

Lenin spoke some truth, but he probably never imagined a world where anybody can instantaneously publish videos and photos or tweet and blog about a politician from a mobile phone. Freedom of the press can serve the interests of the few, but then it wouldn't be free would it? The power of the freedom of the press is in the freedom of the people to individually and collectively voice their opinion so as to sway and influence polices which affect the communities they live in and share common interests with. The power of the freedom of the press allows individuals, institutions, and media outlets to share information that provides for the public good, such as through notices of dangerous weather conditions or in the form of directions to an immunization clinic. Ultimately Lenin had it wrong, but it is still up to the people to ensure the press stays free, not just of government or corporate persuasion, but also of the type of slanted bias that creates confusion, mistrust, and contempt for others.

Taliban - U.S. Info War
First published in *The Independent* newspaper

"Our goal with radio is to reach the locals and inform them about what's going on," Thomas Castillo, Moriarty High graduate, explained during a phone interview from Afghanistan on Sunday.

Castillo said what he does isn't necessarily part of a psychological operation, but more of an information program designed to help out the locals.

"There is an election coming up in the province," Castillo said. "We're broadcasting messages telling them where they can vote."

Castillo is an information technology specialist in the Army, where he spends his days keeping the network up which carries Army radio broadcasts to locals.

Castillo said the broadcasts aren't just for propaganda, but admitted they do serve as a counter measure to the information released by the Taliban.

He said Pfc. Bowe Bergdahl, an American soldier who is currently being held hostage by the Taliban, is from his brigade. He said he is aware of the recently released Taliban video showing the captured American, but said he hasn't watched it.

"They don't let us look at anything like that. They shun us away from it," he said.

In the video Bergdahl is questioned in English. The interrogator asks Bergdahl if the U.S. government informs the public that the U.S. military is working with warlords accused of violating human rights.

"No our government does not inform us of any of these details. They don't tell us any of that specific information," Bergdahl says in the video.

Castillo said leaflets are being dropped by the U.S. asking people to help locate the hostage. He did not say if radio broadcasts were being used to try and locate him as well.

"If we do have to put out an IO message," Castillo said, "we put out the IO message, and after that we consult with the locals in the region to figure out the best way to handle it. And we pretty much go from there."

Castillo said he isn't "specifically going out to spend time with individuals that hear the messages."

Most of the interaction, he said, is done by the Provincial Reconstruction Team, which also works on providing humanitarian assistance in the area.

Castillo said "it's just as easy for them [Afghans] as anybody else" to have access to information, as long as they can afford it.

"They listen to BBC more than any local stations," Castillo said.

In a 2005 School of Advanced Military Studies report by Maj. Peter Sicoli it states that two of the five "significant challenges that negatively affected the Army's IO plan in post-hostility Iraq" was proliferation of news sources and use of the media.

In Afghanistan the situation may be different, but the Taliban hostage video confirms that there is an information war going inside (and outside) the country, which Castillo is also partaking in by maintaining the equipment that disseminates the information.

A typical work day for Castillo begins at 9 a.m. After arriving at work Castillo checks to see if anything is wrong on the network. When there are no problems people will occasionally ask questions about things like programming errors. Castillo is out of the office by 9 or 10 p.m. and will then do laundry, watch a movie or play X-Box.

"Our local area is pretty secure," Castillo said. "We don't really receive any incoming [fire]."

He said another nearby forward operating base where the Afghan army and police are trained gets hit frequently. Castillo thinks the targeting may be selective.

"If I had to say anything I think it's because the fact that the teams here, aside from us and COD teams, are mainly reconstruction teams that go out and help the locals."
He said that about 30 minutes away "you have IEDs and you have small arms fire. It's all depending on your area."

Castillo said the country has a long of history of war, but progress is being made to create a lasting peace. He said it is important to eradicate corruption in the political and legal system and thinks those that are actually fighting in the country are a small group.

"That small group will phase out and die off and we'll have people in the cities more accustomed to living in a peaceful manner," Castillo said. "That's going to take a while to develop."He said all the U.S. can do is push the country in the right direction, but it is up to the people to decide if they are willing to go in that direction.

Castillo advises that Americans "stop reading into the media and grab a couple books about people who have been out here and read about what they've been through."

He said he is proud of his brother and sisters and misses his friends and New Mexican food.

"Tell everybody that I love them," he said.

Fri Jul 24, 2009 | 08:57 AM |

After Note: Bowe Bergdahl was still MIA as of 11/30/2012.

Veterans Integration Center to Receive $100,000 (press release)

The New Mexico Veterans' Integration Center will receive a $100,000 check from the Jean E. Owens Charitable Remainder Trust Fund tomorrow, Aug. 4, at 5:30 p.m.[11]

The Integration Center provides shelter for homeless veterans and families and offers healthcare screening, counseling and job training skills for less fortunate veterans.

The trust fund will also donate $100,000 to the Rio Grande Chapter of the Blue Star Mothers and $100,000 to the All Faiths Receiving Home for Vulnerable Children.

Another $100,000 will go to the St. Jude's Children's Research Hospital in Memphis. Judy Owens and Meredith Lawrence will present the check at the center. The trust fund was created by them after their father, Dale Owens and mother Jean passed away.

Dale Owens was a Navy Lieutenant Commander who served in the Korean War and later became president of Esso Standard Sekiyu Oil Company.

Mon Aug 3, 2009 | 07:45 PM |

Post 9/11 GI Bill - Some Iraq/Afghan Vets Lose Out

The New Mexico Department of Veterans Services' Secretary John Garcia will discuss the Post 9/11 GI Bill on KKOB AM-770 on Monday, Aug. 10 from 9 a.m. to 9:50 a.m. Garcia will take calls and answer questions during the session.

The bill, which went into effect Aug. 1, will pay for the college education of veterans who served after Sept. 11, 2001. In New Mexico 3,100 veterans are currently using the existing GI Bill. More than 30,000 veterans in the state have served in Iraq or Afghanistan.

The Post 9/11 GI Bill was created for people like me who served in Iraq after 9/11, but for those of us who have already used our existing GI Bill we won't receive the full benefits of this bill. Once all Montgomery GI Bill entitlements are used, eligible veterans can apply for the Post 9/11 GI Bill but can only receive up to 12 months of benefits.

So anyone who served after 9/11 and got out in 2004 or before that went straight to school on the old GI Bill will lose thousands of dollars in benefits for taking the initiative to get an education. This is a real bummer for folks like me who had to supplement the old GI Bill with student loans to pay for school. I served from 2000 to 2004, deployed three times, twice to Iraq, got shot at and risked my life for an unpopular war only to return to find out I won't receive the full benefits of a bill that was created for people just like me simply because I got an education as soon as I got out of the military. If only I had lolly-gagged around for a couple years instead of going to school!

What I propose is that the government pays the difference for the cost of benefits lost due to this oversight. The new GI Bill's monthly housing allowance is equal to the monthly payments of the old GI Bill. So basically I should get four years of the new GI Bill without a housing allowance. Right now I will only get one year with the housing allowance.

It is a shame that this bill did not cover those of us who were already in school. It's not like there were very many of us (see the above numbers) already using up the old GI Bill while the new one was being created. This just goes to show that if you sit around and let legislators make these bills without saying anything they will simply forget about you, even if the legislation is supposed to be for you!

Fri Aug 7, 2009 | 01:26 PM |

After Note: A report on the New York Federal Reserve website states that U.S. student loan debt was approaching $1 trillion in early 2013, the second largest balance of household debt after mortgage debt.[12] Why does the government allow financial institutions to squeeze every last dime out of students' pockets and then raise the interest rates when the job market is so fragile? The cost of higher education is starting to weigh more than the benefits, especially when considering how easy it is to get free educational material off the internet, including video lectures of professors from prestigious universities like Harvard.[13] Why should anyone get tens of thousands of dollars worth of loans so they can go to a second rate college when they can get something even better for free? The cost of the degree doesn't seem to be worth it when nobody's hiring. I say clean the slate for outstanding student loan debt for people in low paying career fields who are at least halfway toward their retirement, freeze the interest rates on all owed student loan debt for out of work graduates actively seeking work, create new government positions for college graduates out of work after one year of graduation to prevent work skill atrophy and to improve hireabilty in the private sector, provide government student loan consolidation and debt relief programs for college graduates having a hard time meeting minimum monthly payments on their debt, and invest more in K-12 public education and the future of the United States.

Ben Ray Lujan's Comments on His Visit to Iraq & Afghanistan

New Mexico Rep. Ben Ray Lujan recently returned from a trip to Iraq and Afghanistan where he met with members of the N.M. National Guard and officials in the region including General Stanley McChrystal, the commander of U.S. Forces Afghanistan and NATO's International Security Assistance Force (ISAF), Afghan President Hamid Karzai, and Ambassador Karl Eikenberry, a United States diplomat to Afghanistan.

Here is what he said upon his return:

"It was also important to have discussions with officials in Iraq and Afghanistan about the situation on the ground," said Rep. Luján. "President Obama has outlined clear withdrawal dates in Iraq – with a goal of withdrawing all combat troops by August 2010. The benchmarks are being met, and the Iraqis are beginning to take responsibility for their own country. These are positive steps. Although I believe that President Bush never should have invaded Iraq in the first place, it is important that we support our troops as they continue this withdrawal. I will be following developments in the country closely, especially the withdrawal of troops to make sure that we are reaching our goals."

"The situation in Afghanistan is difficult; we never should have taken our eye off the threat in Afghanistan by invading Iraq. There is violence in the southern region, and the drug trade is still strong - feeding the Taliban with money that allows them to fund their violent activities which are preventing global peace," said Rep. Luján. "With that said, it is important for the American people to have a report presented to them, a comprehensive report that outlines a clear strategy and goals for Afghanistan. That is why I supported the McGovern bill calling for such a report to Congress. There is still much work to do in the country, and the Afghan people have to be committed to establishing a democracy in their country, addressing human rights, education and eradicating drug production. We can work toward these goals with the 42 nations who have committed support."

In June, Rep. Luján voted in favor of an amendment that would have required the Secretary of Defense to provide Congress, by the end of the year, with an outline of its exit strategy for U.S. military operations in Afghanistan. The amendment was considered as part of the FY 2010 National Defense Authorizations Act (H.R. 2647). The amendment failed by a vote of 138 to 278. There was a similar standalone bill introduced earlier by Rep. James McGovern (D-MA), HR 2402, which Rep. Luján cosponsored.

I agree that a clear exit strategy should be developed and understood by our elected officials and members of the military. It needs to be understood by the soldiers on the ground and the American public what the goals of the U.S. and allied military forces are and how these can be accomplished. As I understand it the goal is to eradicate the Taliban and al Qaeda while also rebuilding the country's infrastructure and political structure. Correct me if I am wrong because I don't recall ever having been told what the U.S. and allied forces exact goals are. I'm not sure the above mentioned goals can be accomplished in the near future and suggest that we reassess these goals to make sure if they are truly beneficial to the American people.

In the meantime there is a larger war being waged on terrorists, drug dealers and international crime syndicates worldwide. Although the wars in Iraq and Afghanistan (and Pakistan) may be important pieces to winning the war on terrorism, I'm unconvinced that a military (and diplomatic) victory in those countries will ultimately be a victory against terrorists.

As I have said in the past, I believe the U.S. and allied military forces should reposition themselves throughout the globe in order to combat terrorists in more areas, while simultaneously delivering a massive psychological (or information) operation in order to convince current and future enemies of the western world that a diplomatic solution can be reached. I believe the U.S. military is doing a good job in waging war and think a short-term military victory can be accomplished in Afghanistan, and think one has already been achieved in Iraq, but the long-term diplomatic victory we need for a long sustaining peace cannot be won through violence and warfare, although there is a role for the military in this goal.

To all the boots on the ground in Iraq and Afghanistan: Keep up the good work! To all the civilians, elected officials, and the general population: Let's put our heads together and figure out a solution so we no longer have to live in fear of terrorism or even our own police and military. The bloodshed has to stop for us to be able to move forward and evolve together as a united species.

Fri Aug 14, 2009 | 02:44 PM |

Marine Corps Ban on Social Networking Not 21st Century Warfare

From "U.S. Marine Corps Bans Social Networking Sites" (*BusinessWeek*): *Citing security concerns, the United States Marine Corps has issued an order banning access to social networking sites like Facebook, MySpace and Twitter on its network for the next year. The Pentagon is now reviewing its social networking policy for the entire Department of Defense.*

The reason for the ban? Too much personal information is leaked and the potential for hackers to break into military networks is too great. Okay, I see the potential security threat, but the Marine Corps' solution should not be the final say. Social media sites are the frontlines of the information war being fought in this battle of ideologies against violent radical extremists and the democratically free society of the western world which seeks peace and security for itself and the rest of the world. Banning Marines from being able to fight this war is not 21st century thinking.

Every Marine should be encouraged to find and communicate with as many people as possible in order to explain why the United States is doing what it is in the war on terror. Marines should specifically target the younger audience of the Middle East and Africa where the youth are exposed to a barrage of anti-American propaganda. In communicating to this audience the Marines will not only counter the propaganda, but they can also persuade this population to become allies rather than foes in this war.

Perhaps a ban is in order to figure out exactly how the Marine Corps can launch this type of operation in an effective matter and to figure out how to better protect their own networks, but a permanent ban will only prevent the rest of the world from knowing why they should take sides with the Marine Corps in their fight against global terrorism.

Tue Aug 18, 2009 | 05:56 PM |

After Note: Marines are allowed to use social media sites now, and the Corps even has a social media handbook called "The Social Corps, U.S.M.C. Social Media Principles" which explains how Marines should properly communicate online.[14] The Marine Corps made the right decision by doing this and although my stance on the use of military media campaigns has changed since I wrote this post, I do think the Marine Corps will do a much better job winning hearts and minds through media campaigns than through bombing campaigns. The pen really is mightier than the sword.

Veterans Integration Center to Move to Value Place (press release)

The New Mexico Veterans' Integration Center will move to the Value Place Hotel at 6101 Central Avenue where 55 rooms will be set aside for veterans and their families. The current facility houses about 70 veterans.

"This will mean a significant upgrade for the veterans and their families," said John Garcia, secretary of NM Veterans Affairs. "The Integration Center will continue its mission to serve these families, but in a bigger and more modern facility."

New Mexico has about 7,000 homeless vets. There are about 180,000 veterans in the state. A Memorandum of

Understanding will be signed at 3:30 p.m., Aug. 31 at the Value Place Hotel and will be attended by Garcia. The Integration Center provides shelter, healthcare screening, counseling and job training for veterans.
Fri Aug 28, 2009 | 07:26 PM |

Remembering the Invasion: The Date Factory

The date factory sucked. We stayed there forever, moving back and forth between the factory and other locations. Our main post was a pistol factory where the Iraqis had been producing Berettas. The place reminded me of some kind of Stephen King novel where all the machines came alive at night. We stayed there for a long time, fixing up the place and being hot.

One night at the date factory, when we were all asleep, sweating and snoring, one of the boots got dumb and pulled the trigger on his M16. The factory came alive after that, but it doesn't compare to the time the Iraqi cop was shot in the throat by one of our own Marines.

We did a lot of security patrols through the city and guarded different areas. We moved along the highways on big five ton trucks. We put sandbags between the cab and the bed of the truck so I could stand there and aim my machinegun from the top of the cab. There was no more shooting for me after this point in the deployment, but there was still action going on. Gunshots could be heard all night while we guarded the pistol factory. I started getting annoyed and decided that a stray would eventually hit me. .
Fri Aug 28, 2009 | 07:37 PM |

Note: The following poem was written while standing guard along the highway near Fallujah during my second deployment to Iraq, this time with 2/1, Echo Company. For more poetry on chaos and war check out *Technipoems*, a self-published book for sale at lulu.com/spotlight/scottalbright.

Desert Dream
Sitting by the highway in this burning sun.
In this desert heat.
This never ending sand that whips across our faces.
Loneliness concocts daydreams of other places.
Staring out into the waste, it's hard times and survival from food so tasteless.
Give me water. Liquid for my soul.
Give me hope. Lift me from this hole.
Take away these ants & flies. The mosquitoes, these lives.
These people so willing to die.
Just another job. A task to be done.
Draining my strength. I no longer feel young.
We must secure these roads, the paths people travel.
All of us being branded & herded like cattle.
This language of babble.
But it connects us, let's us talk and reminisce.
Speak of the loved ones and the families we miss. Tell of the things for which we all wish.
The days seem never ending. The night is dark and dangerous.
Isn't there a way to rearrange this? To change this?
To make it better for all of mankind? Shorten up the time.
What has to be, that's all, that's just life.
I guess that's just fine.
Some people complain, bitch and whine.

What's yours is yours is, and what's mine is mine.
Let me be until I get away from right here.
Tomorrow will come shortly after the sun sets.
So God please guard me from fear.
Let me live. Let us all, so we can go home.
So I can read my mom this poem.
So these bullets and bombs will leave me alone.
Fri Aug 28, 2009 | 07:40 PM |

Martin Heinrich on National Defense

On August 24 I sat down with New Mexico District - 1 Rep. Martin Heinrich for a 30 minute interview where I asked questions about defense, drugs, healthcare and education. The interview was conducted for *The Independent* newspaper, which ran a short article I put together for the paper. The following is a partial transcript of the recording from that interview.

*(SA=Scott Albright, MH=Martin Heinrich).

SA: I want to start off with the war in Afghanistan. Currently a lot of the commanders are saying that we need to increase troop levels even more there. So I'm wondering what is your position on that? Do you want to see more troops or not?

MH: "I think in the long term I want to see us out of Afghanistan but I think we have a responsibility to leave there in a responsible way and to stabilize the situation in Afghanistan and to work with their government to get a handle on security before we depart. I'm very pleased to see the draw down in Iraq being on schedule and I think that will give us some flexibility to address some of the security issues in Afghanistan. So it's not an ideal situation. We kind of let that whole mess fester for a number of years and I think it's going to require some intensive attention, and my hope is that by giving that attention to it now it will actually shorten the time period to when we can bring all of our troops home from Afghanistan."

SA: Do you have a number of troops in your mind that you think would be necessary to accomplish the mission in Afghanistan?

MH: "No. I've been in conversation with the leadership that comes and speaks in front of the House Armed Services Committee. I was briefed by Secretary Gates and Secretary Clinton before leaving on the August break and I think they're utilizing an adaptive approach. As a civilian I'm not going to come up with a magic number that's not based in reality. I think the key is giving it the kind of attention it should of had six years ago, eight years ago so that we can bring some stability, train the Afghans and enable them to provide their own security.

SA: Representative James McGovern introduced an Afghanistan exit strategy bill. Do you support this bill and why or why not?

MH: "I voted for a similar measure when we were going through the appropriations process and it simply said that we should have an exit strategy for Afghanistan. I think that in any conflict overseas that we're involved in that we have to think about what are the goals? What does meeting those goals actually look like and then how do we get out afterwards? I think it's a mistake to spend years not defining what victory looks like. So I think it's very important to have an exit strategy whether you're talking about east Africa in the 1990's, or Iraq in the early 2000's, or Afghanistan today. I think that's a very important part of being able to not only bringing our troops home, but to accomplish a logical set of goals."

SA: So you didn't really answer if you would. . .

MH: "I would support the legislation, yeah. The provision that we voted on was fairly close to the legislation."

SA: Can you kind of explain what your role is in the House Armed Services Committee and also what you do in terms of regulating defense spending?

MH: "In terms of defense spending we just passed an overhaul of procurement process and that was a long bipartisan effort trying to get costs down within the defense industry. We were able to get that out of committee with strong support on both sides of the aisle."

"In terms of my role specifically on armed services there are a couple subcommittees I sit on. One is called Readiness, and one of the things it does is it creates the military construction list of priority projects. So, for example, we were able to see $5.8 million in funding secured for the space development test wing here at Kirtland through my efforts on that committee. Kirtland is beginning to be a real focus for cutting edge space technology and activities - everything from space weather and the new facilities going in out there to . . . I'll call it the weather that impacts our satellites and things like that to Operationally Responsive Space, which is about creating satellites cheaper, faster."

"I would say that if you ever heard the story about how we spent a lot of time and effort and a lot of money trying to develop a pen that would write in zero gravity space and the Russians just used pencils. That's kind of what ORS is about. It's about rather than having these hugely expensive, incredible satellites that can do 100 things perfectly, sometimes it's more responsive to the needs we have to do 80 percent of that really well and have something that costs a tenth as much. So there's some really exciting stuff going on at Kirtland as a result."

"The other committee that I sit on is called the Strategic Forces Committee. It deals largely with policies surrounding spacecraft, satellites, strategic weapons systems ranging from the nuclear deterrent to missile defense. It deals directly with the Department of Energy and NNSA activities that go on at Sandia National Labs. So it's a good place for me to be in working with Sandia and what's important for New Mexico in terms of jobs to be on that Strategic Forces Subcommittee."

SA: So were you essential in getting some of this funding for, I guess Kirtland just recently tested a TACSAT-3 and their calibrating that right now?

MH: "Yes, that's part of the ORS program."

Heinrich explained how he helped to get a new mission for the Air National Guard's 150th Fighter Wing at Kirtland Air Force Base:

MH: "Without being on armed services it would have been very difficult to do that work. We were able to get language in both the defense authorization bill and the defense appropriations bill to tell the Air Force that before they retire this wing they have to come up with the next mission and figure out a transition plan. That's important work that we could not have done - it would have been very difficult to do that not being on one of the committees of jurisdiction."

SA: Do you think spending on weapons procurement is beneficial to national security or does it add fuel to the fire of the international arms race?

MH: "I think it depends on how you administer those dollars. I don't want to spend money just to spend money. I want to spend money to secure our national defense. We need to do a more effective job of making sure those dollars are spent as effectively as possible. We see the importance of this if you look at the conflict in Iraq. It took us a number of years to get vehicles that were safe for our soldiers and our Marines in Iraq. Today we have the MRAPs that are fantastic because they survive IED explosions and they effectively protect our troops. The vehicles that we were sending our soldiers and Marines out with six years ago in my opinion were not a good use of the dollar because they weren't designed to protect those men and women, or they weren't effective at protecting them. It's not just about the dollar amounts it's about spending those dollars wisely and making sure we get the outcome that we want."

Sun Aug 30, 2009 | 06:05 PM |

No Need for High Unemployment Rate Among Vets

From "Veterans unemployment rate hits 11.3%" (*Marine Corps Times*) by Rick Maze, posted Friday Sep 4, 2009 17:39:12 EDT:

"The number of unemployed Iraq and Afghanistan veterans is now almost the same as the number of service members currently deployed in support of those two wars, according to new Labor Department numbers.

A key member of Veterans of Foreign Wars said the data indicates that the government needs to do more to help separating combat veterans find jobs and that veterans need to think about their options, including using the improved GI Bill to attend college while also getting a living stipend,.

Labor Department figures released Friday show the nation's unemployment rate has now reached 9.7 percent — the highest in 23 years — and the rate among Iraq and Afghanistan veterans is 11.3 percent.

About 185,000 Iraq and Afghanistan veterans are out of work, just 9,000 fewer than the number currently deployed to those two areas, said Justin Brown of the VFW's national legislative service."[15]

MY TAKE: Why isn't the federal government going to the men & women getting out of the service and offering them jobs? I would have signed up to do just about anything except another enlistment after getting out of the service. The feds could've sent me off to Timbuktu for all I cared. I just wanted a civilian job. I was single, well trained, proved I could hold a job for four years, young, and ready to take on the world. Had I been snatched up by any number of federal agencies to go work in the civilian sector I would have been more than happy and I would've gone just about anywhere. It's crazy that the feds, as well as private companies, aren't waiting in line to get their hands on fresh, strong, disciplined servicemen about to join the civilian sector. What a waste of good talent!

Now that I've been out for almost five years I'm a lot pickier about what I'll do. I refuse to be sent off to some war torn, dangerous location, and I'm sure not going to work 75 hours a week for minimal pay. I would have five years ago, but not now. So why aren't the public and private sector bustling to get their hands on these talented young men and women coming back from Iraq and Afghanistan? The article says because of the competition, but there's more to it than that.

After getting out of the service and receiving my bachelor's degree I still couldn't find much work. So here I am struggling to get by with a huge student loan debt because the Montgomery GI Bill didn't pay nearly enough. I've decided to go for my masters because I'm confident the investment in my education will eventually pay off. I'll only quarlify for 12 months of the new GI Bill and will still be stuck with a stack of student loan debt without much help from the government. So here we are: a bunch of well trained, educated, disciplined, unemployed veterans who still aren't getting the help we need.

The solution: HIRE A VET! States: GIVE VETS FREE EDUCATION! HELP PAY OFF VETERANS' STUDENT LOANS! MAKE HEALTHCARE A PRIORITY FOR RETURNING VETS AND THEIR FAMILIES! STOP SPENDING STIMULUS MONEY ON THE SAME OLD CONTRACTORS AND PASS IT ON TO THE VETS THAT DESERVE IT! RETRAIN VETERANS FOR FREE! OFFER TECHNICAL SCHOOL PROGRAMS THAT HIRE UPON COMPLETION!

One of the worst things a country can have is a bunch of highly trained killers running around without jobs: The U.S. is not Russia in 1991, but. . .

Fri Sep 4, 2009 | 09:34 PM |

Albuquerque Conference for Women Vets (press release)
Date/Time: Saturday September 12, 2009 (8am)
Location: Albuquerque Hilton Hotel
Cost for the event is $15. Pre-registration is strongly encouraged.

A representative from the NMDVS Education and State Approving Agency will discuss education opportunities and benefits—especially the new Post-9/11 G.I. Bill.
Job-training and apprenticeship programs and opportunities will be discussed and a representative from the NMDVS Veterans' Business Resource Center will highlight benefits

and services offered through the NMDVS Veterans' Business Resource Center (VBRC).

Staff from the Raymond G. Murphy VA Medical Center in Albuquerque will also be there to talk more about available veterans' medical benefits and services

For more information and registration, call Christin McKinley at (505) 459-0367.

Sat Sep 5, 2009 | 07:19 PM |

Agent Orange Linked to Parkinson's Disease (press release)

Veterans of Foreign Wars (VFW): "Agent Orange Linked to New Diseases

"In its recent review of medical research into the long-term effects of exposure to herbicides in Vietnam, the Institute of Medicine (IOM) concluded that there is a suggestive link between exposure to Agent Orange and Ischemic Heart Disease, Parkinson's Disease and certain rare cancers.

In the same review, the IOM affirmed its earlier conclusion that there is a significantly increased risk of developing hypertension in those who served in Vietnam.

The Veterans of Foreign Wars is calling on the VA to fully recognize these findings and award presumptive service connection for veterans suffering from these diseases who were exposed to Agent Orange.

In 2000, a similar study found a link between Agent Orange and Type II Diabetes. Those findings led the VA to recognize presumptive service connection for Vietnam veterans suffering from the disease.

"Based on this data, the VA should take swift action," says Gerald Manar, Deputy Director, National Veterans Service. "The VFW is pushing for full recognition of

conditions linked to Agent Orange exposure, along with proper medical care and timely compensation."

MY TAKE: It is far too late to provide timely compensation for those who have been exposed to Agent Orange!
Thu Sep 10, 2009 | 02:52 PM |

Below: A picture of a sign hanging in the hallway at the VA hospital in Albuquerque.

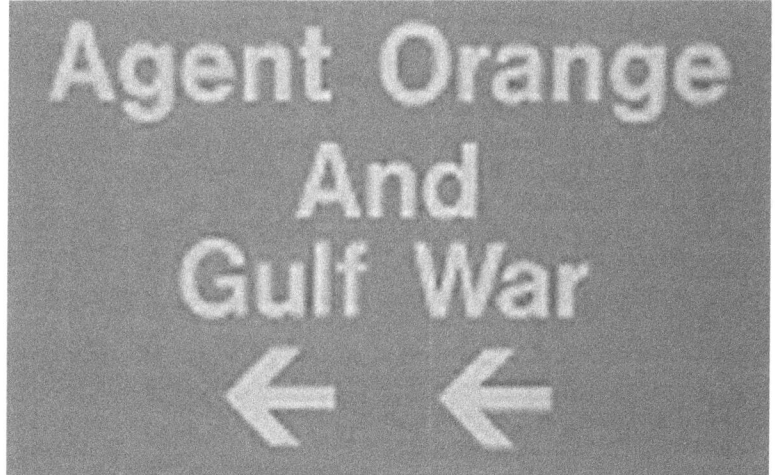

CHAPTER 4 NOTES

1 *The Independent* published an edited version of the article published here. For the edited version see Albright, Scott. "Moriarty graduate helps Afghan radio," *The Independent*, July 9, 2009.

2 Jakes, Lara. "Marines: More Afghan soldiers needed in Helmand," The Associated Press in *Marine Corps Times*, July 8, 2009. http://www.marinecorpstimes.com/news/2009/07/ap_marines_helmand_0 70809/.

3 Faiez M. Karim and Laura King. "Attack on U.S. base in eastern Afghanistan kills two soldiers," *Los Angeles Times*, July 5, 2009. http://articles.latimes.com/2009/jul/05/world/fg-afghanistan5.

4 Faiez M. Karim and Laura King. "GI apparently seized in Afghanistan," *Los Angeles Times*, July 3, 2009. http://articles.latimes.com/2009/jul/03/world/fg-afghanistan3.

5 Warden, James. "'First with the truth,'" *Stars and Stripes*, May 5, 2009. http://www.stripes.com/news/first-with-the-truth-1.91202.

6 Radio Free Europe. "Gunman Said To Kidnap 16 Afghan UN Workers," Radio Free Europe Radio Liberty, July 5, 2009. http://www.rferl.org/content/Gunmen_Said_To_Kidnap_16_Afghan_UN _Workers/1769900.html.

7 See www.veteranscourt2.net for more on New Mexico's Veterans Court. Also see Brunt, Charles D. "New Court To Target Troubled Veterans," *Albuquerque Journal*, October 31, 2011. http://www.abqjournal.com/main/2011/10/31/news/new-court-to-target-troubled-veterans.html. For more information on veterans courts visit the Center for State Courts Veterans Courts Resource Guide webpage http://www.ncsc.org/Topics/Problem-Solving-Courts/Veterans-Court/Resource-Guide.aspx.

8 See *The Jakarta Post*, "Police bomb squad combs hotel after explosion," July 17, 2009. http://www.thejakartapost.com/news/2009/07/17/police-bomb-squad-combs-hotel-after-explosion.html.

9 Graff, Peter. "U.S. condemns video of soldier captured in Afghanistan," *Reuters*, July 19, 2009. http://in.reuters.com/article/2009/07/19/idINIndia-41149520090719.

10 Walker, Martin. *Powers of the Press,Twelve of the World's Influential*

Newspapers. New York: The Pilgrim Press, 1983, pg. 138.

11 Visit http://www.nmvic.org/ to learn more about the New Mexico Veteran's Integration Center.

[12] Lee, Donghoon. "Household Debt and Student Debt," February 28, 2013. http://newyorkfed.org/newsevents/mediaadvisory/2013/Lee022813.pdf.

[13] Harvard Extension School. "Harvard Open Courses: Open Learning Initiative," Harvard University. http://www.extension.harvard.edu/open-learning-initiative.

[14] See http://www.marines.mil/Portals/59/Docs/Marines-Social-Media-Handbook%5B1%5D.pdf. On page 8 it states Marines are allowed to express political views on public issues or political candidates online, but not as part of an organized communication campaign. What in the world does that mean? Unorganized communication campaigns should be all right then. Just keep your political views as chaotic as possible when communicating them online.

15 Maze, Rick. "Veteran's unemployment rate hits 11.3%," *Marine Corps Times,* Sept. 4, 2009. http://www.marinecorpstimes.com/news/2009/09/military_veterans_unemployment_090409w/

DEMILITARIZING SPACE:
HOW MEDIA AND NON-STATE ACTORS CAN RESTRAIN U.S. AND PRC MILITARY ACTIVITIES IN OUTER SPACE

BY SCOTT ALBRIGHT

Scan the QR Code to read
the abstract and buy
a copy of Scott Albright's
graduate thesis
Demilitarizing Space

5| SPACE LASERS & PATRIOTS

Colonel Michael Duvall Explains Laser Technology

Colonel Michael Duvall, Base Commander for the 377th Air Base Wing, Kirtland Air Force Base, explained how laser technology can be used to take out a missile while speaking at a Sept. 11 breakfast at the Embassy Suites Hotel. Duvall talked about the different divisions and agencies at the base to a crowd of military men and community members, while also remembering the 9/11 attacks.

In an economic impact statement distributed at the breakfast it states that KAFB expects a $59 million economic impact in the next two years from mission growth. Growth from the Air Force Nuclear Weapons center is expected to create an economic impact of $22 million. The money will go towards payroll and local job creation. Other areas expected to generate monies from mission growth are in the AFRL Battlespace Environment Division ($22 million), 377th Security Forces Squadron ($11 million), and the Air Force Inspection Agency ($4 million).

Duvall said the base plays an important role in developing and testing new technologies involving directed energy, space weather, satellites, and spacecraft.

Kirtland coordinated with other agencies to help launch a new satellite, known as TacSat-3.[1] Different payloads are being tested on the satellite including the Advanced

Tactically Effective Military Imaging Spectrometer hyperspectral imager, built by Raytheon, Satellite Communications Package from the Office of Naval Research, and the Air Force Research Laboratory's Space Avionics Experiment.

According to Duvall the satellite will be able to detect the difference between fake grass and real grass, but it may not be effective against IEDs.

Sat Sep 12, 2009 | 06:02 PM |

Bill Richardson to Speak At POW/MIA Ceremony

New Mexico Governor Bill Richardson will be the guest speaker at Kirtland AFB's 2009 Prisoner of War/Missing in Action Recognition Ceremony at the New Mexico Veterans Memorial, Sept. 18 at 10 a.m. Before the ceremony Airmen will participate in a 24 hour run and vigil at the Hardin Field parade ground on base.

Thu Sep 17, 2009 | 12:16 PM |

Medal of Honor: Jared Monti

President Barack Obama presented the highest military decoration, the Medal of Honor, to the parents of Army Sergeant First Class Jared Monti during a ceremony in the White House last week. Monti was killed during a firefight in Afghanistan when his 16-man patrol was ambushed by about 50 Taliban fighters. During the firefight Monti risked his life to rescue a wounded soldier and was cited for his courage.

Monti is only the second U.S. soldier who has received the medal for service in Afghanistan. Four soldiers and Marines have been awarded the medal for service in Iraq.

The following is the full text of the citation as listed at history.army.mil[2]:

*MONTI, JARED C.

Rank and Organization: Sergeant First Class, United States Army. For conspicuous gallantry and intrepidity at the risk of his life above and beyond the call of duty: Staff Sergeant Jared C. Monti distinguished himself by acts of gallantry and intrepidity above and beyond the call of duty while serving as a team leader with Headquarters and Headquarters troop, 3rd Squadron, 71st Calvary Regiment, 3rd Brigade Combat Team, 10th Mountain Division, in connection with combat operations against an enemy in Nuristan Province, Afghanistan, on June 21st, 2006. While Staff Sergeant Monti was leading a mission aimed at gathering intelligence and directing fire against the enemy, his 16-man patrol was attacked by as many as 50 enemy fighters. On the verge of being overrun, Staff Sergeant Monti quickly directed his men to set up a defensive position behind a rock formation. He then called for indirect fire support, accurately targeting the rounds upon the enemy who had closed to within 50 meters of his position. While still directing fire, Staff Sergeant Monti personally engaged the enemy with his rifle and a grenade, successfully disrupting an attempt to flank his patrol. Staff Sergeant Monti then realized that one on his soldier was lying wounding in the open ground between the advancing enemy and the patrol's position. With complete disregard for his own safety, Staff Sergeant Monti twice attempted to move from behind the cover of the rocks into the face of relentless enemy fire to rescue his fallen comrade. Determined not to leave his soldier, Staff Sergeant Monti made a third attempt to cross open terrain through intense enemy fire. On this final attempt, he was mortally wounded, sacrificing his own life in an effort to save his fellow soldier. Staff Sergeant Monti's selfless acts of heroism inspired his patrol to fight off the

larger enemy force. Staff Sergeant Monti's immeasurable courage and uncommon valor are in keeping with the highest traditions of military service and reflect great credit upon himself, Headquarters and Headquarters Troop, 3rd Squadron, 71st Calvary Regiment, 3rd Brigade Combat Team, 10th Mountain Division, and the United States Army.
Sat Sep 19, 2009 | 05:22 PM |

Rep. Ben Ray Lujan Rejects Afghan Troop Increase

New Mexico Rep. Ben Ray Lujan sent out a press release today explaining his position on troop levels in Afghanistan. In the release, and in a letter to President Barack Obama, Lujan states that he is "concerned about becoming involved in a long-term counterinsurgency that requires hundreds of thousands of troops."

"We need to give support to the Afghan people through humanitarian and diplomatic means, but troop increases are troubling at this time," Lujan continues. "I urge the Administration to reject a troop increase."

Lujan represents district three, which covers Santa Fe and northern New Mexico.

Rep. Martin Heinrich, who represents Albuquerque and central New Mexico, said during an interview with me last month that he is in favor of increased troop levels. Heinrich did not specify how many more troops should be sent to Afghanistan, but he suggested an increase would help to accomplish the U.S. and NATO mission in the country.

Both Heinrich and Lujan are in favor of legislation that would provide a clear exit strategy.

Lujan does offer some suggestion on how to deal with international terrorism. The following is a snippet from the letter he sent to Obama:

"We support your administration's declared goals of defeating Al Qaeda and reducing the global terrorist threat. But, we believe that adding even more U.S. troops to the military escalation that your administration ordered in March would be counterproductive. We urge you to consider and pursue the full range of alternative options including applying the lessons of the Cold War where we isolate and contain those who pose a threat to our national security."
Fri Sep 25, 2009 | 01:08 PM |

G-20 Protest Raises Questions on Use of Force

Protestors at the G-20 Summit in Pittsburgh faced off with the military and riot police. Tear gas and non-lethal weapons were apparently used against the protestors. A YouTube video shows men in fatigues forcing a protestor into an unmarked car.[3] Although I understand the concern for security and the safety of summit members, I do not see the reason for such a huge police presence.

The protests in Pittsburgh bring up questions about the use of force by such a police and military presence: What happens if a real attack occurs and riot police shoot a bunch of protestors? If you were in uniform would you be able to shoot on Americans? What would the public reaction be?

I can't predict the future, but I think a lot of people would be pretty pissed.
Sat Sep 26, 2009 | 10:02 PM |

"Control Room" Slant Not Credible

I just finished watching "Control Room", a movie about Al Jazeera's coverage of the Iraq war, and felt the need to make a few points.[4]

First off, the U.S. military did use propaganda to influence the media and there was a bit of a show for the cameras, as when I was in Fallujah and the general was paying a visit to our location. Before the general's scheduled visit we were all joking and smoking, making the best of our situation, but just before the general was to arrive we all took up posts throughout the area we normally wouldn't have stood security at and made sure everybody was awake and looking good. Yes, we put on a dog and pony show for the general, just like the military PR guys put on a dog and pony show for the media, but how can that possibly be a surprise to anyone? The U.S. did not want journalists revealing the true nature of war, as was the case in Vietnam, because mom and pops can't stand to see the true gore of the battlefield, and images of dead children does not work in favor of an invading force.

What surprised me about the movie Control Room is that these journalists did not report about those who did greet us in the streets with clear optimism. In one part of the movie it talks about how children screaming god damned Bush in Arabic was translated into them cheering for Bush, but the fact is kids would come up to me and say in English "good Bush, good." We would get smiles and waves, and offered tea, and were well accepted in many parts of the country. Control Room pretends like this never happened. Also, they say men were brought in for the media to parade around the main square in Baghdad to provide images of jubilant Iraqis freed from their oppressor. Perhaps this is true, I was not in the square at that moment, but I do know that the men, women and children who were celebratory where I was at were not hauled in. They emerged from houses and buildings and lined the streets in many different parts of the country. Of course there were those that openly disapproved of the U.S. military who shouted profanities and threw stuff at us, but Control Room does not explain this in their movie.

The other thing that I keep hearing over in over is that Americans should have controlled the looting in Baghdad, as if this was a major turning point in the war. I've heard people say that the U.S. should have been more brutal and stomped down on all looters in order to show who was the dominate force, but this is total BS. The only way the military could've controlled the looters was to shoot or bomb them. The Marines were not in any way ready to go out and be riot police upon arriving in Baghdad. The Marines were ready for warfare, not riot control. Had Marines turned on the looters with their guns it would have made the situation far worse.

The fact is the U.S. military did try to stop the looters, but there were far too many Iraqis running amuck and far too little troops to chase them all down. Think about this: if the LAPD couldn't stop their own people from looting and ransacking the streets of Los Angeles during the LA riots, why would anyone expect an occupying force to stop people from looting their own country?

I have the utmost respect for the journalists who risk their lives trying to get accurate information for the world to see, and appreciate Al Jazeera's efforts to show another side of the war, but Control Room shows how Al Jazeera's media bias was simply inaccurate.

Sat Oct 10, 2009 | 06:34 PM |

Free Clothing, Food, Counseling For Homeless

Homeless veterans and non-veterans received free clothing, toiletries, food items, counseling, flu shots, health care, legal advice and dental care at the New Mexico Veterans' Integration Center today, Oct. 23.

The VA estimates there are about 7,000 homeless veterans living in New Mexico.

Where I live I see two to three homeless people sleeping in the park each day. It's about time we give them the help they need. Thank you NM Veterans' Integration Center for reaching out to non-veterans during this year's stand down.

It's getting colder here in New Mexico and many of the homeless who sleep in the park will find their way into diners, busses, public libraries, and other places to stay out of the cold. Instead of shooing them away like pests, let us provide what we can and at the very least be kind and give some guidance as to where they can go to get food, a warm place to sleep, and help with alcohol and drug addictions.

The homeless of America are people too and should be treated humanely and with compassion. It is a shame that we have let so many men and women who have served this country, and even those who haven't, wander the streets. It is always the right time to help those in need.

Fri Oct 23, 2009 | 08:19 AM |

Military Service is all about Helping the Community
First published in *The Independent* newspaper

"The message I want to send to the kids is about service – not necessarily in a combat zone – but community service," Chief Warrant Officer 4 Lawrence Jiron said during a Veterans' Day event at East Mountain High School.

Jiron was among more than 30 veterans who came to speak to students at the high school on Monday.

"We're excited to have so many people come out and talk," EMHS Prinicpal Doug Wine said. "It is important for the students to know what Veterans' Day means historically and what it means personally."

Students assembled around the flagpole and applauded the veterans before the national anthem was played on an electric guitar by senior Jeffrey Delanoy.

A moment of silence was given to the families that were affected by the recent shooting tragedy at Ft. Hood and senior Kayla Skye Allmon gave a speech to honor veterans and military personnel.

As part of her service learning project, which all seniors must do at EMHS, Allmon is collecting donations and toiletry items for troops deployed in Iraq and Afghanistan. Anyone interested in donating can call the school at 281-7400.

After the ceremony around the flagpole students went back to their classrooms to listen to the veterans, many of whom have served throughout several conflicts and wars, speak about their time in the service.

Students in room 206 asked questions about working in the military to Jiron and Army Pvt. Brice Leinnewebe. Both Jiron and Leinnewebe have family members who attend EMHS. Jiron's son, Lorenzo, was able to listen to his father answer the questions asked by fellow students in room 206, while Leinnewebe's sister, Danika, was in a different classroom.

Lcinnewebe just finished basic training in the Army where he works as a mechanic. He told students that it is his passion to work on vehicles and that the Army allowed him to pursue his dream.

One student asked what the two service members' proudest moments were. Leinnewebe said his proudest moments were graduating basic training and coming back home to his family, while Jiron said his proudest moments were being in the classroom talking to students and providing for the community.

By being in the Army Jiron has been able to help on search and rescue missions in New Mexico and served in Louisiana after Hurricane Katrina where he set up communications lines that had been destroyed from the storm.

"It's about helping people in our own state and in our own country," Jiron said.

While in Afghanistan, Jiron also provided humanitarian assistance by providing food, medicine, and school supplies to the locals.

Jiron told students that if they join the military they should do it to serve their country and community and not for the benefits.

When asked about how difficult it is to carry heavy gear all over the place Leinnewebe said "it's one big mind game," to which Jiron said "you get used to it," and agreed that with Leinnewebe that "it's all in the mind."

Leinnewebe and Jiron both said one of the challenges of being in the military is always having to "hurry up and wait."
Wed Nov 11, 2009 | 01:59 PM |

Note: I moved to Hawai'i in December 2009.

Big Island Love (First post from Hawaii)
Aloha from the big island. Sorry all or the lack of recent posts. Looks like Yemen and Somalia are in the headlines again. Who would have guessed? But the question is still out there: how to win hearts and minds? Can you change the beliefs of violent extremist with force? The answer is

diplomacy but can the international community step up to the plate?

Tue Jan 12, 2010 | 08:45 PM |

Top Weapons Exporters
From SIPRI Data 1989-2003
Downloaded SIPRI Data show that Russia and the USSR are ranked as two of the top five exporters for 1989-2008.[5] China ranks seventh but is the second largest importer of weapons following India for the same time period. The majority of Russian exports are to China. China's largest buyer is Pakistan. From the data it is obvious that the U.S. is the largest weapons producer and exporter, and therefore the least credible when it comes to setting standards and creating nonproliferation policy. All five permanent members of the U.N. Security Council are major proliferators and are also the least likely of nations to create a real binding nonproliferation policy. Perhaps the best strategy would be to ask the leaders of countries who export and import the least amount of weapons to decide policy. But that's probably un-American of me to come up with such a preposterous idea. I just think somebody needs to take the lead on arms reduction that can actually be trusted and not seen as a hypocrite.

Mon Feb 22, 2010 | 01:34 PM |

Iraq War Vets Blog Changing Names
I'm considering changing the name and focus of the blog and want some feedback from the readers. I want to have a broader international perspective but don't want to proceed in changing the format without some insight. It seems appropriate to discuss issues regarding international security

rather than just veteran's issues and the wars in Iraq and Afghanistan.

The U.S.' war on terror has expanded to Pakistan, Somalia, Yemen and other parts of the world and global cooperation has become a distinctive factor in the military's success. Cooperation between NATO forces and other international organizations is the key to reducing terrorist activities, but discussion on this topic has been limited in the media in my opinion.

The Shanghai Cooperation Organization rarely makes it in the news and India's joint military operations with Southeast Asian countries seem to be overlooked. I want to discuss some of these issues in greater detail, so please post some responses and let me know which direction I should take this blog. Thanks.

Fri Feb 26, 2010 | 04:15 PM |

Controlling the Media in the Digital Age

A recent search of the National Security Archive database on Iraq led me to a document titled "Rapid Reaction Media Team" Concept, which provides an outline for the U.S. government to provide training and infrastructure to Iraqi journalists.[6] The information in the document isn't surprising, but it provides some insight into how the U.S. government has done its best to control and influence the flow of information.

I reported earlier about the Marine Corps' decision to ban the use of social media sites and recommended the military reverse this strategy in order to promote democracy worldwide by providing the type of information necessary to create allies in the war against terrorism. In some respects I support the idea of psychological operations in social media, however only for purposes beneficial to the human race at large. The DoD did reverse their decision, but have limited the talk on social media to subjects that will not disrupt national security (okay by me.) For more information on this read CNN's "U.S. military OKs use of online social media."[7]

One of the most interesting aspects of the digital age is the ability for people all over the world to express their opinion on subject matter of any type. It's hard to say how much influence government or any other major media outlet can have on public opinion because of the numerous amounts of views publicized in the media.

I've been particularly interested in the government's ability to influence privately owned media corporations and have been trying to find as much as I can on Operation Mockingbird, an operation that allegedly ties the CIA to some of the most prominent media conglomerates in the world. In today's world can any government, corporation, or other entity really control the flow of information? Hackers in China get around the Great Firewall every day. Is it even in the interest of government to control information anymore? I would argue that restricting the free flow of information only dumb-down populations and prevents people from becoming more prosperous.

For more on Operation Mockingbird check out the conspiracy theory website Prison Planet.[8] And if anyone has a more reliable source on this operation please post a response. Thanks.

Mon Mar 1, 2010 | 03:32 PM |

Election Day Can Prove Democracy Works

Looks like Iraq is heating up again. A string of bombs went off throughout the country during early voting on

Thursday.[9] Most of the voters were police and security personnel who must work on Election Day. Several other attacks were prevented, according to news reports.

Preventing violence during and after elections is the key to making the democratic system work. Some say Iraq isn't ready for democracy and that it shouldn't be shoved down their throat, but I disagree and think this year's election can be the proof in the pudding, but violence must be deterred for it to be successful.

Although the United States may be focused on many things at once, i.e. healthcare, Afghanistan, spending bills, jobs, etc., Iraq needs to be a main point of focus for the Obama administration and the U.S.'s allies. Every time the United States goes to war, creates a new government, and then abandons the country the rest of the world looks on in dismay. No one wants to use the United States as a model for their own political system if this is what democracy really looks like.

Providing Iraqi's with the support they need during this election is just the beginning of a long road toward a democratic relationship between the United States and the Middle East that, if worked properly, can lead to peace. By providing security support, election monitoring, suggested election ethics laws, and by inviting Iraq into the global community and international organizations the United States can be successful in reaching its goals of creating a democratic Iraq. I'm sorry to say that war had to be waged for us to get to this point in Iraq and believe it was not necessary, but I am happy that Iraqis now have the opportunity to pick and choose who they want their leaders to be.

With some luck and hard work, violence will be deterred, corruption will be avoided, and people will be happy with the leaders they select to represent them.

Fri Mar 5, 2010 | 02:09 PM |

Obama's Commitment

"So thanks to you, there's been progress these last several months. But we know there are going to be some difficult days ahead. There's going to be setbacks. We face a determined enemy. But we also know this: The United States of America does not quit once it starts on something. You don't quit, the American armed services does not quit, we keep at it, we persevere, and together with our partners we will prevail. I am absolutely confident of that." - Obama to the troops in Afghanistan.

Obama looked pretty drained giving this speech. He kept looking down at his notes and was not nearly as charismatic as he usually is. Is this a sign of his confidence on the mission in Afghanistan? I sure hope not, but to give the above statement shows his determination. This could be a really, really, really long war, because the problem the United States faces is not only in Afghanistan. Terrorism is a worldwide phenomenon and as long as there is a war against it, there will be a soldier to fight in it.

Hopefully the war on terror, the war on drugs, and the war on crime will all see an end, but I'm highly doubtful. One day humans will evolve and act civil toward one another, but for now we must live in this constant state of war.

Mon Mar 29, 2010 | 04:36 PM |

Side Note: The U.S. is scheduled to withdrawal all U.S. troops from Afghanistan by the end of 2014.

Biofuel for U.S. Military Green Fleet

The *Big Island Weekly* ran a story about the U.S. military's idea to buy up land in Hawaii in order to grow crops for biofuel. The biofuel would in turn be used to power military vehicles and aircraft.

In the story an antiwar activist named Jim Albertini was quoted as saying, "Instead of growing food to feed the island's population, we're going to be growing fuel to feed the military's war machine."

Doesn't Albertini understand that what's feeding the war machine is oil? The U.S. is the largest consumer of oil in the world, and the American military uses as much energy as the whole country of Nigeria![10] If the military "goes green," than that's a great start.

Thu Apr 22, 2010 | 04:20 PM

After Note: I have since met and talked with Albertini a few times. I respect his position and think that his commitment to peace and active engagement with the community through protest and demonstration is exactly what is needed to keep Americans informed about the realities of what the U.S. military does overseas. An online article by Andrew Walden in the *Hawai'i Free Press* blasts Albertini for his anti-military positions and previous criminal convictions. Apparently Albertini was convicted of felony charges for jumping into Hilo bay to block the USS Ouellet nuclear armed- warship from docking in what is legally a nuclear free zone.[11] Albertini is right to be concerned about the military use of both nuclear and biofuel technologies. It is my hope though that the military's pursuit of alternative fuels can help to re-orient and convert the military industrial complex and its financial organs from a war-driven industry to an environmental and humanitarian-driven one, where peace-based mission directives are the norm and wars and violent conflict are extremely rare.

Positive Images

I recently replaced the header picture on this blog from a machinegun pointed at Fallujah to a more positive image (I'm still deciding). The reason I did this is because I don't want people to see the image of a machinegun and think this blog is about promoting war and violence. For me the machinegun image represented a state of mind after returning from war, but I no longer have the desire to live with this mindset. When I first came back from Iraq I was always on high alert, ready to move out, re-deploy, or take action against an enemy. My machinegun was always loaded and ready to fire, even if it was just in my head. After nearly six years of being out of the military I've finally unlearned many of the things I was programmed to do, and I'm thankful for that.

I don't want to be on high alert all the time, or to be worried about the possibility of being blown up or shot at. I don't want to feel like I have to look over my shoulder all the time, and now I don't, well at least most of the time. After six years I've finally begun to feel normal, but for many returning vets normal will never come again. I've met Korean War vets who still deal with these issues, and there are thousands of Vietnam vets across America who constantly re-live the nightmares of their war.

It's time to take a break. The U.S.' military adventures have created a society of paranoid war veterans, and here we are, still doing the same crap. America continues to send people like me off to war before our brains are fully developed - before we even have the ability to understand what the consequences of war really are. And the consequences are devastating. Not just for the people it was waged against or the country it was waged in, but also for the soldiers who partook in the violence. Luckily American troops are being treated much better today than they were after Vietnam, but the television, radio, newspapers, and magazines constantly bombard the American public with stories of the horror, the violence, the crimes, and the killing. These things did happen, and they are important to tell about it in order to prevent it from happening in the future, but there are good soldiers and Marines with good intentions that did everything right in the war, yet they still feel guilty for the crimes that were committed. They shouldn't have to.

I'm not saying to only focus on the good and to hide the truth about the U.S. military. I'm not saying this at all. What I am saying is that the military does good things, and can do even more. The military is here to stay whether you like it or not, so instead of resisting it, do something to make it better. When I joined I was enthralled with the idea of being one of the few and the proud to serve my country and to help others around the world. I thought I would become self-disciplined, morally responsible, and physically healthy. I wanted to join in on the humanitarian missions across the planet and I wanted to be able to do something good for the world. Unfortunately I found that Marines were as corruptible as anyone else, that self-discipline can't be programmed into you by someone else, and that the moral dilemmas of war are much harder to deal with than the moral dilemmas of civilian life. I didn't instantaneously become what I imagined I would through the Marine Corps, but I learned some valuable lessons.

I learned that war is awful, that it will torture the soul, and that life is a blessing. I pray that the world can see peace, and hope that the military can help to bring it, not through more bombs and missiles, but through intelligent solutions. For now I will let you all think about the possible solutions until I decide to post again.

Signing out from the Big Island,

Scott Albright

Mon May 10, 2010 | 03:53 PM |

Alien Takeover

Okay I changed my header again. So how does this reflect my mindset? I'm not sure, but I figure aliens must have something to do with all the war this world goes through. Are humans really biologically inclined to kill one another? I don't think we are.

What is the purpose of the military anyway? Is it to take over and control other countries in the name of that military's national interest? Maybe the military's role is not for the purpose of securing national security. What if its real purpose is to secure corporate security? Think about. Do civilians really have control of the military? Are those fat cats in Washington really listening to their constituents when military policies are addressed in Congress? Most of the time the general public is left in the dark about these issues, and if people are informed they don't seem to give a damn. Maybe it's because the real power lies within the corporate lobbyists who spend so much on campaign contributions in order to prop up the military industrial complex that politicians will listen to no one else. How can the average middle class American even compete with the lobbyists who can throw money around to support one bill or another? Meanwhile

CEO's earn major profits while the sons and daughters of the middle class go off to spill blood in order to keep their company's interests secure.

It seems impossible to me that this is really a human system. These corporate mongrels are jeopardizing our children's futures. Let's re-examine where the United States is headed and do something to change it.

Tue May 11, 2010 | 01:11 PM |

On Humanitarian Aid

The following is a section from a term paper about humanitarian aid and disaster relief programs in China.[12]

The most important aspect of the aid program I recommend would be for the immediate disbursement of aid in times of need. There would be pre-constructed channels of delivery for humanitarian relief materials through U.N. peacekeepers and military alliances such as NATO, the SCO, the African Union, and others. Each alliance would be responsible for distributing the aid to their regions of operation. For example, the SCO would be responsible for providing aid to Russia, China, and Central Asia, NATO to Europe and North America, the African Union to African countries, and so forth. Because it is the military which have the best equipment for delivering such aid, and can provide the type of security needed to disburse materials once on the ground, it is these militaries which should be delegated the duties of providing aid.

Restructuring these militaries to be the most efficient and cooperative for such operations would need much work, but I believe it could be done through negotiations among U.N. members. By restructuring militaries and military alliances to focus on disaster relief efforts as their main objectives, the world could benefit as a whole because the politicization of security issues in the name of national interests and natural resources would become secondary to the objective of providing disaster relief and humanitarian assistance. The purchasing of disaster relief materials and deciding which disasters would require the most attention are other considerations the U.N. must think about before such a program could become effective, but those issues will not be addressed here.

Tue May 11, 2010 | 01:21 PM |

Cooling Pyongyang

As the United States military combats terrorism in Iraq and Afghanistan a new threat looms in the distance. News articles report that North Korea will wage an all out war with South Korea if Seoul attempts to punish Pyongyang for the sinking of the Cheonan warship which was allegedly hit by a North Korean torpedo off the coast of the Korean peninsula. North Korea denies the attack and China, a longtime ally of Pyongyang, has remained silent on the issue, while North Korean leader Kim Jong Il recently returned from a trip to Beijing this month.

What does all this mean for the United States and the 25,000 plus American soldiers stationed in South Korea? North Korea will not be allowed to get away with the sinking of the ship, but South Korea does not want to provoke a war. So how can Pyongyang be punished without sparking conflict? And does any action by Seoul or the western powers really make a difference to North Korea? Any sanctions, military retaliation, or intelligence gathering by South Korea and the west probably will not deter Pyongyang from committing a similar type of act in the future, and it may just further provoke the north.

Secretary of State Hillary Clinton is on her way to Japan, South Korea and China, and will undoubtedly be pulling all the diplomatic strings she can to resolve the issue peacefully, but no matter how hard she pushes for a resolution someone will be trying to screw it all up, whether it's a right wing extremist in the United States, or a Pyongyang hardliner. She must not give in to pressures from the Pentagon to rush toward a military response, and she must not let Beijing set the course for the negotiations. China's role in easing tensions over North Korea's aggression is vital, but it is too often the case that American diplomats give way to Beijing's demands without getting anything in return. This is not a situation where South Korea will just let China "take care of it", and if Clinton returns without any resolution, Seoul may take things into their own hands.

Although North Korea is usually more bark than bite, this situation could escalate if not managed properly. The United States should not be alone in asking Beijing to cool its neighbors' aggressive tendencies and direct talks with Pyongyang should be held through the United Nations, with all members of the Security Council involved in the talks.

An all out war between North and South Korea could make Iraq and Afghanistan look like a baby's playpen. Both North and South Korea have advanced military capabilities, and when the United States, China and other countries get thrown in the mix it is understood that all out war in Asia could mean all out war worldwide. Hopefully Clinton will be able to pull out some magic tricks on the other side of the Pacific, but she cannot do it alone. Clinton will need the full support of the Obama administration in her attempts to ease

tensions, and hopefully the rest of the world will be right beside her in trying to keep the peace.
Thu May 20, 2010 | 01:44 PM |

"Come on, you sons of bitches, do you want to live forever?"
Never mind the M.A.S.H. theme song; suicide is not painless. According to Eric Shinseki, director of Veterans Affairs, of the 30,000 suicides each year in America, about 20 percent are committed by veterans. A quick Google search will reveal many articles about suicide rates among Iraq and Afghanistan war veterans, and surprisingly the number of suicides by these veterans may outnumber the total amount of combat deaths. WHAT IS GOING ON?
Here's a report of the most recent suicide that took place today:
From NPR's Democracy Now!:
Iraq War Vet Commits Suicide at Ohio Military Hospital
"An Iraq war veteran has committed suicide in front of a veteran's hospital in Dayton, Ohio. Jesse Charles Huff shot himself with a rifle in front of the Veterans Affairs Department's Medical Center last month. Huff had been denied unspecified treatment at the hospital just hours earlier. The father of Huff's former roommate says he thinks Huff killed himself in part to make a statement about the inadequate medical care he received as an injured veteran. Huff was wounded by a bombing in Iraq and had been undergoing treatment for a back injury and depression." [13]

There seems to be a lack of data to help explain why suicide rates among Iraq and Afghanistan war vets are so high, but one can make a list of possibilities: financial problems, relationship issues, depression, drugs (including prescriptions), the feelings of guilt left behind from the war, and other personal issues. Whatever the reason, it is obvious that more needs to be done. Let me wrap my brain around this issue and try to come up with something that can be done.

While in the military service members have to think about surviving. The military does a great job of instilling this drive for survival. One must kill or be killed. As Sergeant Major Daniel Joseph "Dan" Daly said, "Come on, you sons of bitches, do you want to live forever?" But once out of the military this need to live forever is no longer pounded into the heads of the men and women who saw all the horrifying events that go along with being in combat. The media, family, and friends can put new messages into the heads of these young veterans, who will often times question their role in the war after hearing about the heinous nature of the invasion and occupation. The feelings of guilt will hack away at the minds and souls of veterans who no longer have a vested interest in killing or fighting. Drinking, drugging, and other misbehavior will seem like innocent fun compared to the horrors of war, but one misstep and a veteran can land in jail, or worse; tormented by a loved one for something stupid they did. The punishment will seem out of place. For how can a vet be locked away or tortured by a spouse for something so menial compared to what they did in Iraq or Afghanistan? How can a veteran justify the killing when that is obviously worse than what they are punished for as a civilian? To many the answer is suicide. But wait, this isn't an answer at all.

Suicide does not fix the problem. Life does not get better for those left behind and the misery can carry on through death, or into the next life. Besides the emotional wreck suicide causes for loved ones, there are funeral costs to consider, past debt and bills, and children left without a mom or dad. The possibility that life could get better is lost forever. No, suicide is not painless.

So how should this issue be addressed and what can be done to eliminate suicide among veterans? I'm not an expert in this field and I don't claim to have a good answer, but I'll throw out a suggestion. For me there was never any time to think about suicide while in combat. If I was going to die it was going to be from someone else's bullet, and I sure as hell wasn't about to let that happen. If it came down to me or them I was determined to make sure it was them. One can learn from this mentality. Of course veterans don't want to be in a combat state of mind as civilians, but there is something to this state of mind that can benefit one's drive for life and survival. My suggestion is that veterans who have the urge to end it all consider rekindling this survival mode and combat mentality. Don't let anyone convince you that you're less than you really are. You survived combat right? Surviving in garrison is much easier. Just catch some of Dan Daly's spirit and you may just be able to live forever.

Tue May 25, 2010 | 02:48 PM |

Memorial Day: A Time to Hire Vets

I received an email today asking me to support S. 3234: Veteran Employment Assistance Act of 2012.[14] I quickly responded by sending a letter to my local representatives. Please check out the links to learn more about the bill and to see how you can help get it passed. Also check out the following links to find out about employment services for military veterans: Recruit Military, Vet Jobs, Jobs4Vets, Military Hire, and Hire Heroes USA.[15] These are just a few of the sites that popped up when typing in "jobs for vets" in Google's search engine. Services are out there and people are putting in the work to get veterans employed, but it's still not enough.

A chart presented by the Bureau of Labor Statistics website shows that Gulf War II veterans (post-Sept. 11, 2001) were more likely to be unemployed in 2009 than nonveterans, but veterans who served in other conflicts or time periods were more likely to be employed than nonveterans.[16] Other data show that younger veterans are more likely to be unemployed than older veterans.

The Department of Labor states that unemployment among veterans is not much different than that of nonveterans, but the data clearly shows that Gulf War II era veterans are more likely to unemployed than nonveterans.

According to the Iraq and Afghanistan Veterans of America website, unemployment rates among Iraq and Afghanistan veterans is a serious problem. The site quotes the Bureau of Labor Statistics as saying that unemployment for Afghan and Iraq war vets was at 14.7 percent for March, 2010. According to the Bureau of Labor Statistics website, the national unemployment rate for April, 2010 was 9.9 percent.[17] According to the same website, the April, 2010 unemployment rate for Gulf War II era veterans (Afghan and Iraq wars) was 13.1 percent.[18] For information on veteran employment for 2009 see: http://www.bls.gov/spotlight/2010/veterans/home.htm.

It is obvious that veterans who served in Iraq and Afghanistan are less likely to be employed than nonveterans or their older veteran counterparts. Things are being done to change this, but there is still more work to be put in. Younger veterans have experience in handling some of the most advanced high-tech equipment in the world. Many have trained or managed small work units and have an extremely good work ethic due to the high demand of the military. These veterans are some of the best trained and most disciplined in the entire world, yet they are having a harder time finding a job than nonveterans. This doesn't make any sense. The longer a veteran is unemployed the easier it is to lose some of the good work ethics and skills learned while in the military. That is why it is important to find work for these veterans immediately after completing their service contracts. Of course most servicemen and women want a break after getting out of the military and they deserve it, but that doesn't mean they all have to be receiving unemployment benefits.

Employers who seek military veterans as employees should be given incentives to provide transition training for new hires. Incentives should include tax breaks, federal and state transition training assistance, and public recognition for their commitment to veterans and their country. Employers should be on base knocking down doors to hire these new veterans. Veterans who are serious about their future should not ignore these employers as they prepare to exit from the military. Yes, there is time to play after being discharged, but if playtime doesn't equal pay time, than quit having fun and get back to work or take advantage of the new GI bill and go to school. An unemployed veteran doesn't have to become a homeless veteran. There are opportunities out there!

Fri May 28, 2010 | 11:59 AM |

Showing Respect on Memorial Day

President Obama won't be laying the wreath at the Tomb of the Unknown Soldier at Arlington National Cemetery this year. He will be attending a Memorial Day ceremony at the

Abraham Lincoln National Cemetery in Illinois instead. Vice President Biden will attend the ceremony at the Arlington Cemetery. So why are so many people fussing about this? I say stop bitching about the president and respect the holiday! Obama is not the first president to not attend the ceremony at Arlington and I'm sure he won't be the last. This is a day to give thanks and respect to American servicemen and women for the sacrifices they have made for the United States of America, not a day to bitch about the president.

Despite the military-industrial-complex's motives and the bullshit politics behind America's wars, the people who have actually done the fighting are the ones who spill the blood and sweat to make the U.S. military the toughest in the world, and they deserve the full respect of the country for doing this. What they don't need is a bunch of whining babies complaining that the president isn't at some ceremonial event. If people want to complain about the Commander and Chief's role in the military, then complain that he is not on the front lines in Afghanistan or Iraq sitting in a fighting hole ordering troops to advance on the enemy. That's what a strong leader who really believes in the war would do. That's what George Washington did and that's what I think all presidents should do if they are in office during war time. If you want to complain about something then there you go, but to bitch about something as simple as laying down a wreath? Come on. Get a life!

Out of respect for the servicemen and women who are deployed overseas, and for all the other Americans who have served the country, I have posted President Obama's Memorial Day proclamation:

Presidential Proclamation--Memorial Day
"Since our Nation's founding, America's sons and daughters have given their lives in service to our country. From Concord and Gettysburg to Marne and Normandy, from Inchon and Khe Sanh to Baghdad and Kandahar, they departed our world as heroes and gave their lives for a cause greater than themselves.

On Memorial Day, we pay tribute to those who have paid the ultimate price to defend the United States and the principles upon which America was founded. In honor of our country's fallen, I encourage all Americans to unite at 3:00 p.m. local time to observe a National Moment of Remembrance.

Today, Americans from all backgrounds and corners of our country serve with valor, courage, and distinction in the United States Armed Forces. They stand shoulder to shoulder with the giants of our Nation's history, writing their own chapter in the American story. Many of today's warriors know what it means to lose a friend too soon, and all our service members and their families understand the true meaning of sacrifice.

This Memorial Day, we express our deepest appreciation to the men and women in uniform who gave their last full measure of devotion so we might live in freedom. We cherish their memory and pray for the peace for which they laid down their lives. We mourn with the families and friends of those we have lost, and hope they find comfort in knowing their loved ones died with honor. We ask for God's grace to protect those fighting in distant lands, and we renew our promise to support our troops, their families, and our veterans. Their unwavering devotion inspires us all -- they are the best of America.

It is our sacred duty to preserve the legacy of these brave Americans, and it remains our charge to work for peace, freedom, and security. Let us always strive to uphold the founding principles they died defending; let their legacy continue to inspire our Nation; and let this solemn lesson of service and sacrifice be taught to future generations of Americans.

In honor of their dedication and service to America, the Congress, by a Joint Resolution, approved May 11, 1950, as amended (36 U.S.C. 116), has requested the President to issue a proclamation calling on the people of the United States to observe each Memorial Day as a day of prayer for permanent peace and designating a period on that day when the people of the United States might unite in prayer. The Congress, by Public Law 106-579, has also designated 3:00 p.m. local time on that day as a time for all Americans to observe, in their own way, the National Moment of Remembrance.

NOW, THEREFORE, I, BARACK OBAMA, President of the United States of America, do hereby proclaim Memorial Day, May 31, 2010, as a day of prayer for permanent peace, and I designate the hour beginning in each locality at 11:00 a.m. of that day as a time to unite in prayer. I also ask all Americans to observe the National Moment of Remembrance beginning at 3:00 p.m. local time on Memorial Day.

I request the Governors of the United States and the Commonwealth of Puerto Rico, and the appropriate officials of all units of government, to direct that the flag be flown at half-staff until noon on this Memorial Day on all buildings, grounds, and naval vessels throughout the United States and in all areas under its jurisdiction and control. I also request the people of the United States to display the flag at half staff from their homes for the customary forenoon period.

IN WITNESS WHEREOF, I have hereunto set my hand this twenty-eighth day of May, in the year of our Lord two thousand ten, and of the Independence of the United States of America the two hundred and thirty-fourth.

BARACK OBAMA

Fri May 28, 2010 | 12:57 PM |

Bingaman Supports the Veteran Employment Assistance Act

The following is the email reply I received from NM Sen. Jeff Bingaman after contacting him about the Veteran Employment Assistance Act. Anyone who cares about the American economy should support this bill. Please contact your representatives to let them know how you feel.

"Thank you for contacting me regarding veterans. I appreciate your taking the time to write. As you may know, S. 3234, Veteran Employment Assistance Act, was introduced by Senator Patty Murray on April 20, 2010 and was referred to the Senate Committee on Veterans' Affairs. This legislation would provide entrepreneurial training and counseling to veterans; federal assistance to small businesses owned and controlled by veterans; a training allowance for each month that an unemployed veteran is enrolled in a full-time employment and training program; and allow the use of veterans' post-9/11 educational assistance for the pursuit of apprenticeships and on-job training. I strongly believe that it is our government's responsibility to provide our Nation's service members and veterans with the services and care that they deserve, and please be assured that I will keep your letter in mind as this issue is discussed in the Senate.

Again, thank you for writing to me. I encourage you to continue to inform me of issues of importance to you and your community."
Sincerely,
JEFF BINGAMAN, United States Senator
Phone: (202) 224-5521
Toll-free in NM: 1-800-443-8658
Website: http://bingaman.senate.gov/
Mon Jun 21, 2010 | 10:03 AM |

Deterring North Korea through a Show of Force: RIMPAC & the F-22

From June 23 to August 1 fourteen nations will be jointly conducting military operations in the biennial Rim of the Pacific (RIMPAC) exercise in and around the Hawaiian Islands. This year the United States will be showcasing some of the 20 new F-22 Raptors to be stationed at Hickam Air Force base. The jet is one of the most advanced fighter planes in the skies, fitted with stealth technology that can allow it to slip behind enemy lines at supersonic speeds of up to 1,000 miles per hour. Two squadrons are already based at Elmendorf Air Force Base in Alaska and several of the planes have deployed to Guam and Okinawa in the past as a show of American support to U.S. allies in the Pacific. The RIMPAC exercise and the new jets come just four months after a South Korean warship was sunk off the Korean peninsula. An international report indicates that the South Korean ship was split in two by a North Korean torpedo.

RIMPAC, along with the new fighter jets in Hawaii, are not only thought to be deterrence to North Korea, but also as a show of force to other potential adversaries in the region like China. Xinhua news reports that China is urging restraint over the current military exercises. According to one article by the state sponsored news agency, China's foreign ministry spokesman Qin Gang stated it would be of a cold war mentality to conduct joint Chinese - North Korean military exercises in response to U.S. warships in the region. Qin went on to say that "no single country or military alliance can resolve issues like regional security and stability," and that all countries in the region need to work together.

China has done little to help restrain North Korea from provoking war in the region however, and many in China see the U.S. military presence in the Pacific as a threat to the Communist regime. If China wants to genuinely cooperate with the United States than Beijing would have accepted U.S. Defense Secretary Robert Gates' invitation to have closer military relations during his visit to Asia earlier this year. China cut off military-to-military contact after the U.S.' $6.4 billion arms deal to Taiwan in January.

It is unclear what direction China will go in regard to the North Korea issue, but it is widely known that the foreign ministry does not have any say or control over the People's Liberation Army and that any statements coming from the foreign ministry are no more than just wishful thinking. For the sake of the planet I hope that Qin Gang is speaking on behalf of the military as well as the rest of China when he says that cooperation between the U.S. and China is necessary for peace and stability.

U.S. Secretary of State Hillary Clinton and Defense Secretary Gates will visit the heavily fortified DMZ on Wednesday in order to show the importance of American operations there and to demonstrate the U.S.' commitment to providing military support to the south.

Mon Jul 19, 2010 | 04:31 PM |

CHAPTER 5 NOTES

1 NASA. "TacSat-3Inforation," Wallops Flight Facility, Goddard Space Flight Center. Mission update May 20, 2009.
http://www.nasa.gov/centers/wallops/missions/tacsat3.html
2 http://www.history.army.mil/html/moh/afghanistan.html
3 YouTube. "Military Abduction at Pittsburgh G20 Summit!!! Viral! Viral!! Viral!! Uploaded by Kennedy1op, September 24, 2009.
http://www.youtube.com/watch?v=k1IF5ldlUN8.
4 Al Jazeera. "Control Room, Propaganda of the Iraq War," uploaded to YouTube by TheBicycleman79, May 2, 2012.
http://www.youtube.com/watch?v=f3rMo5cgaXQ. Originally released June 18, 2004. Directed by Jehane Noujaim.
5 See Stockholm International Peace Research Institute. "SIPRI's databases." http://www.sipri.org/databases. Click on SIPRI arms transfer database to generate a trade register, importer/exporter TIV tables, and to generate a top list of TIV tables. Also see the SIPRI Military Expenditure Database: http://www.sipri.org/databases/milex.
6 See U.S. Department of Defense, "White Paper – "Rapid Reaction Media Team" Concept," January 2003.
http://www.gwu.edu/~nsarchiv/NSAEBB/NSAEBB219/iraq_media_01.pdf.
7 CNN. "U.S. military OKs use of online social media," March 4, 2010.
http://www.cnn.com/2010/TECH/02/26/military.social.media/?hpt=Sbin.
8 Louise, Mary. "Operation Mockingbird: CIA Media Manipulation," Prison Planet.
http://www.prisonplanet.com/analysis_louise_01_03_03_mockingbird.html. See www.VeteransNotes.weebly.com for a list of suggested reading materials discussing the role of the intelligence community in the media. Although most of the sources I found do not specifically name the CIA's activities involving the media as being called Operation Mockingbird, many sources do provide examples of the CIA and other intelligence agencies' manipulation of the media. For examples of the Mossad's use of the media see Thomas, Gordon, *Gideon's Spies: The Secret History of the Mossad*, Macmillan, 2009, pp. 65, 521, 293, 312, etc.
9 Al Jazeera. "Iraq attacks mar early voting," uploaded to YouTube by AlJazeeraEnglish, March 5, 2010.

http://www.youtube.com/watch?v=WHDS4OVqfPw.

10 Karbuz, Sohbet. "US military energy consumption – facts and figures," *Energy Bulletin*, May 20, 2007.
http://www.energybulletin.net/stories/2007-05-21/us-military-energy-consumption-facts-and-figures.

11 Walden, Andrew. "Hawaii DLNR gives 11 acres to 9-11 truther group," Hawai'i Free Press, September 1, 2010.
http://www.hawaiifreepress.com/main/ArticlesMain/tabid/56/articleType/ArticleView/articleId/2740/Hawaii-DLNR-gives-11-acres-to-911-truther-group.aspx. Also see Jim Albertini's peace vigil leaflet for July 17, 2009, posted at Hawai'i Free Press,
http://www.hawaii247.com/2009/07/14/hilo-peace-vigil-on-friday-july-17/.

12 Albright, Scott. "Suspicious of Humanitarian Aid," China-U.S. Relations website, 2010. http://www.chinausrelations.com/chinaaid.html.

13 NPR. "Iraq War Vet Commits Suicide at Ohio Military Hospital," Democracy Now! May 25, 2010.
http://www.democracynow.org/2010/5/25/headlines/iraq_war_vet_commits_suicide_at_ohio_military_hospital.

14 See govtrack.us. S. 3234 (111th): Veteran Employment Assistance Act of 2010, 11th Congress, 2009-2010.
http://www.govtrack.us/congress/bills/111/s3234.

15 https://www2.recruitmilitary.com/ AND http://www.vetjobs.com/ AND http:\www.jobs4vets.com AND http://www.militaryhire.com/ AND http://www.hireheroesusa.org/

16 Bureau of Labor Statistics. *Employment Situation of Veterans*, "Spotlight on Statistics," May 2010.
http://www.bls.gov/spotlight/2010/veterans/home.htm.

17 Bureau of Labor Statistics. *Economic News Release,* "Table A-5. Employment status of the civilian population 18 years and over by veteran status, period of service, and sex, not seasoanally adjusted."
http://www.bls.gov/news.release/empsit.t05.htm.

18 http://www.bls.gov/news.release/empsit.t05.htm

6| GLOBAL DEMILITARIZATION

Employee Screening For Wartime Contracting a Necessary Procedure

The Commission for Wartime Contracting recently inquired about oversight procedures among some of the top contractors for the U.S. government in Iraq and Afghanistan.[1] The commission asked representatives from five companies (Jul. 26, 2010 hearing - panel 3) about their screening procedures of employees, ethics policies, and subcontracting oversight. The response was mixed among the representatives, but their seemed to be some agreement that screening subcontractor foreign national employees was difficult, if not impossible, within a given timeframe. Most representatives stated that they had some oversight procedure, but most seemed to believe that a complete and formal vetting process of subcontractors and their employees was more of a hindrance than a benefit for mission completion. I agree that screening each individual before being allowed to work on a project is a difficult task but not impossible, and there is no doubt in my mind that better oversight procedures can be put in place to prevent bad actors from engaging in wartime contracting work.

In the book *Merchant of Death, Money, Guns, Planes, and the Man Who Makes War Possible,* authors Douglas Farah and Stephen Braun explain how a lack of oversight allowed world renowned arms dealer Viktor Bout to land contracts for his front companies with the U.S. government in Iraq.[2] Bout's companies would usually be hired as subcontractors to the dirty work for American companies like Kellog, Brown, and Root (KBR):

"The Bout flagship also was a third-tier contractor for the U.S. Air Mobility Command, flying deliveries for Federal Express under an arrangement with Falcon Express Cargo Airlines, a Dubai-based freight forwarder. And Irbis was also flying, Walker learned, under reconstruction contracts with the petrochemical giant Flour, and with Kellog, Brown, and Root, the engineering and construction subsidiary of Halliburton – the influential multinational conglomerate that had been awarded a massive no-bid reconstruction contract in Iraq and that was previously headed by Vice President Dick Cheney."[3] (Pp. 223-224).

Of course Viktor Bout is sitting in a Thai prison after being caught in a sting operation by U.S. officials, but many companies just like his continue to operate worldwide, some of which may still be working for the United States in Iraq and Afghanistan. We cannot single Bout out however; as there are many "bad actors" that have been hired by American companies to do the dirty work in war zones. Many times the bad actors are the ones who have the most experience, the best contacts, and offer the most affordable prices, but that does not mean the United States should continue to work with these people.

The United States cannot instill democratic ideals in countries like Iraq and Afghanistan when the people being used in the reconstruction efforts are thugs and criminals. The message this sends to the people of Iraq and Afghanistan is that America does not care about morality and ethics and that it is okay to be corrupt and criminally associated as long as you are working for Americans. This is the wrong message to send to the people America is trying to help, and it is quite naïve on the apart of American officials to believe these thugs are working exclusively for the United States, as Viktor Bout has proved that loyalty to a political ally is not a necessary requirement for working in war zones.

Loyalty should be dearly considered before awarding contracts to any company working for the U.S. in a war zone. When a company refuses to give up vital records to the Wartime Contracting Commission that could help find out where missing funds have vanished to, it shows that that company is not loyal to the U.S. government, and that they should lose any status they've gained as an efficient contractor. Viktor Bout proved that his loyalty was to money, which seems to be the case with many of the major contractors working in Iraq and Afghanistan today, although they do have a temporary interest in showing loyalty to the mission at hand, but not the overall mission and ideals of the U.S. government.

The best way to prevent contractors from eroding reconstruction efforts through poor oversight of employees and subcontractors is to have a better system of vetting new and old hires. Of course the U.S. government could also limit the amount of outsourcing by keeping projects in-house, but Americans want to prove to the world that privatization and market economies are efficient methods of working in war zones and other places across the globe, so allowing state run agencies to take over the contracting work would also be a backward step in democratization efforts. Screening employees is the key to eliminating the corrupt and criminal elements working for contractors and subcontractors in Iraq and Afghanistan and elsewhere. Of course the screening and vetting of employees, especially foreign nationals, is not an easy task for the prime contractors or the government agencies awarding the contracts, but a coordinated and committed effort by government agencies and contractors to create better oversight procedures will lead to a more streamlined and standard process that will help prevent the problems we see today while also helping the overall cause of the mission.

Wed Jul 28, 2010 | 04:46 PM |

After Note: Viktor Bout was extradited to the U.S. and, despite Russian protests, was sentenced to 25 years in prison for conspiring to sell weapons to a U.S.-designated foreign terrorist group.

Protecting Iraq's Future from the Corporate Vultures

Former U.S. Ambassador to Iraq Christopher Hill spoke at the U.S. Institute of Peace on August 18, 2010 where he talked about the future of U.S. operations in Iraq.[4] During his presentation, which was aired on C-SPAN, Hill discussed the problems associated with the power struggle between central and provincial governments, budgetary issues, the U.S. diplomatic mission, security and other issues.[5] Hill said that despite Iraq's failure to form a government after the March elections, he is sure a power sharing government will be formed and that the possibility of a coup is out of the question.

The formation of the central government is vital to the U.S. diplomatic effort, but more importantly it is the key to building trust among the Iraqi people who still have major concerns about their own security. The longer the leaders take to form a government the more the people will wonder how they can trust the current leaders to provide the necessary services for a prosperous and secure nation.

Without a strong central government to disburse moneys and provide the tools for local governments to provide services to their people the more likely local leaders will challenge the center and attempt to fill the vacuum we are now seeing in Baghdad. The longer the country goes without a formal central government the longer it will take for investors to offer aid to the country.

Hill did address this issue and talked about how important it is for local and national governments to seek investors to provide better services to the people, but he left something very important out. He did not address how these investors can provide the much needed services without placing the Iraqi people in debt. In the book *The Secret History of the American Empire*, author John Perkins discusses how American and multi-national companies tend to pounce on troubled states like vultures in order to make huge profits by offering services like improved electrical and water systems and other basic infrastructure which the states usually have to take huge loans out to be able to afford.[6] Although these services do help the people, it is not the people these companies really care about. What they care about is the profits and the power that comes from keeping countries like Iraq in debt.

Hill discussed the importance of keeping out of the policy making decisions of the Iraqi leadership and explained

how the U.S. has to respect the sovereignty of the country, but he did not explain how this can be done when the country will be in billions of dollars worth of debt to the corporations if they are allowed to provide the type of investments Hill is talking about. Once these investments are made the corporations will basically strip the country of any sovereignty it may currently have. This is the biggest challenge I think Iraq faces today and one that must be addressed by the central government. The nation's leaders have to come together and agree to share power democratically so that they can prevent these corporations from stripping them of their country. It is also important for the United States to help protect Iraq from giving into the corporations which wish to control the countries assets. The Iraqi people must be made aware of how the corporate vultures work and they must band together to create local investments in electricity, water, roads, schools, hospitals, etc. so that they can remain independent and sovereign while still participating in the international system with the assistance and backing of the United States government. It is time for the United States to take a moral stand against the corporate vultures and do what is right in the international community. This is how long term alliances can be achieved.
Fri Aug 20, 2010 | 01:35 PM |

Pentagon Report on China: Factual or Misleading?

An 83 page Pentagon report on China's military was blasted by China's state-run news agencies and the foreign ministry for being inaccurate and unprofessional, yet the Pentagon insists the information in the report is already widely known.[7] The foreign ministry says China's military buildup is for peaceful purposes only, while the Pentagon report suggests otherwise.

The following are a few good links for anyone interested in researching this further:

The Pentagon Report:

www.defense.gov/pubs/pdfs/2010_CMPR_Final.pdf

English Version of PLA Daily: english.chinamil.com.cn

Chinese Version of PLA Daily: www.pladaily.com.cn

Fri Aug 27, 2010 | 01:59 PM |

Boeing to use PetroChina Biofuel in Jets

Comment on *Proactive Investors NA* – "Boeing and PetroChina to asses setting up Chinese aviation-biofuels industry."[8] Although China officially cut off military to military contact with the U.S. after the most recent U.S.-Taiwan arms deal, we can see that military cooperation vis-a-vis private contractors is still ongoing. The above listed article states that Boeing and PetroChina, along with several other companies, are working together to develop biofuels for use in aircraft in which PetroChina provides the biomass and UOP (Honeywell) will process it into jet fuel. (To be used in military aircraft I assume.)

Reporting on this type of cooperation does not make it into the mainstream media because both the U.S. and Chinese governments and state/corporate run media conglomerates want to play Cold War-like games in which the general public is mislead and lied to.

More of this type of cooperation is absolutely necessary for the peaceful evolution of regional military affairs, particularly in the Pacific, and the public should not be led to believe that hostile confrontation between the two superpowers is inevitable. By encouraging a confrontational tone with China the media produces the type of neurologically changing fear that gets people to buy stuff from their corporate sponsors. It is just as important to report about cooperation between U.S. and Chinese companies as it is to report about the disagreements between government officials. Reporting on the positive can lead to more positives which in turn can negate past disagreements.

Fri Sep 3, 2010 | 12:22 PM |

Wounded Warrior - A short story by Rick Albright

She threw me out! What the fuck is that all about? I need her, her sensuality calms my mind, she can't throw me out. I'm too drunk, how much vodka did I drink? About as much as her, probably more, a lot more. She threw me out, the bitch threw me out. Her voice takes me forward and reminds me of what's to come. She threw me out of her apartment, the womb where all is her and her smell that makes me forget. She threw me out. Where do I go, oh yeah, I remember, my place. The empty cave that has been stripped of everything, so when I enter my mind not be reminded of death, nothing to remind me of killing. Where Mr. Vodka is my roomie. Keep walking marine, there is refuge in the cave.

Where the hell am I? I don't remember this field, it is really dark, where are my night vision goggles? I need to see, they're everywhere, I can't see them without my goggles. Maybe this is better who wants to see them shot to bits, who wants to watch the old lady die again? Through the goggles, death on a green screen. Ha ha, the green screen and her white flag of truce. Neither of us were safe. They want to kill me, they want to kill me, I'll kill them first. Careful, carefully, quiet as I can be. Where is my gun? I need my god damn gun if I am going to kill them first. Oh God! Where is my gun? Uh oh, white smoke coming through the metal grid. Gas, put em on, where the fuck is my gas mask? I don't want to die in this god-forsaken desert. Please God, where is my gas mask? Oh shit, I left it at her apartment, and she threw me out.

Easy, easy you are on your way to the cave, just get across the void in this field and it won't be long until you will meet up with Mr. Vodka. He will get you through the rest of the night. He can almost obliterate the dreams, almost, but not like her. Her smell, her touch, I forget who I was and she makes me think of who I can be. Why in the hell did she throw me out? Jesus here comes a car, get down, get down!! They're attacking, here they come, don't fire, hold your fire, fire, they aren't stopping, fire, god dammit fire! They're stopped. What the hell why is the car full of holes? The windows are shattered. What is all that red crap splattered inside? The machine gun is hot, it was only a couple of bursts. Look at those dead kids, you can hardly tell they have faces, that must be their mother. Oh Lord, that is their mother, I'm sorry!! I had to kill you first, don't kill me! There it is, my cave, I hope all the bodies are gone, the charred remains that haunt me, maybe they won't be here tonight. I wish she were here, alright there is Mr. Vodka. Maybe I can sleep, maybe they won't die tonight, maybe they'll leave me alone, maybe they'll stop killing me.

Mon Oct 4, 2010 | 03:07 PM |

2011: The Year of Demilitarization & Weapons Nonproliferation

Here we are bringing in a new year, but not much new has happened in terms of reducing violence and pushing military affairs in a more peaceful and constructive direction.

The START treaty was ratified by Congress and the U.S. and China are rekindling a shaky military relationship, but all in all violence and combat operations across the globe do not seem to be diminishing at the rate necessary for long term peace and cooperation among nations to occur. Gangs, lone gunmen, and drug cartels have been busy in the U.S. and Mexico wreaking havoc on communities while the peace process in Israel has just about fallen apart completely. Muqtada al Sadr's return to Iraq brings new fears of continued sectarian violence between Shiites and Sunnis in that country. Iran is a hotbed for insurgent and terrorist training for rebels in Afghanistan, Iraq, Syria, and Lebanon, while Somalia, the Ivory Coast, Egypt, and several other African nations have seen their share of political and religious violence in recent months. Protests and riots in France and Greece have become so common place it's rarely news anymore, and tensions in the Pacific, around the Korean peninsula, and in other parts of Asia have the world on the brink of war almost 24/7. Predictions by *The Economist* suggest that tensions over Chinese claims to territories throughout Southeast Asia and the Pacific will only increase this year, and it looks like there is no end in sight to the war on terrorism, the war on drugs, or the war on crime being waged by the U.S. and its allies.

It's time for the world to buck up and get these issues resolved, whether it's about territorial claims, religious beliefs, political ideologies, or energy security. We have all become too interconnected to allow violence and war to continue to be a normal part of human relations. War in one part of the world has immediate consequences on the opposite side of the planet, directly and indirectly. By next year the human population will have reached seven billion, while communication and travel between each and every one of us will become all the more easier. As we become more and more interconnected the possibility for total destruction of the human race through war, or the disease, famine, and retaliation that follow, becomes more and more possible, but so does the possibility of everlasting peace. That is why it is time to make 2011 the year of demilitarization and nonproliferation of weapons worldwide. World leaders must unite to refocus their military efforts on providing humanitarian assistance and disaster relief to countries in need, while sharing military technologies in the medical field, communication equipment, and green energy transport with one another, while reducing the amount of money spent on military weapons and combat operations. Instead of slashing the number of troops and the amount of pay and benefits for the men and women who make the sacrifices needed to provide national security and to protect the basic liberties of nations, lets slash the cost of the military budget by reducing the amount of nuclear weapons in every country's arsenal while refusing to provide bacon to the Washington fat-cats who want to bring more weapons development projects to their districts. It's time take waging peace seriously, and one of the ways to do this is to pay attention to and work with our military and political leaders to ensure that global cooperation between nations occurs without building oppressive military alliances and authoritarian power structures. We the people of the planet earth have a right to live peacefully and harmoniously with one another and we the people should demand that our military and political leaders take the steps necessary to ensure that a long lasting peace can be provided to all, no matter where we live. HAPPY NEW YEAR TO ALL!

Mon Jan 10, 2011 | 09:49 AM |

Dealing with the PTSD Demon
Edited version first published in *The Independent* newspaper, Edgewood, N.M., Jan. 19, 2011.

In the summer of 2004 I was in Fallujah, Iraq where I was sniped at, bombarded with rockets and mortars, and threatened by the possibility of being blown up by an improvised explosive device on a daily basis. In the Fall of 2004 I was attending classes at the University of New Mexico where it was the students who were bombarding me with their anti-military rhetoric and anti-war propaganda. The transition from war zone to peace zone was quite dramatic, but the peace my fellow students understood was not the same type of peace I knew.

Since returning home some very tragic events occurred in my life, including the death of a former squad member who committed suicide after struggling with PTSD as a civilian. Another Marine who was in my company, who I am still very close with, is prescribed several types of medication by the VA for his PTSD, including psychotropic drugs, sleep aids, and downers. Other war veterans diagnosed with PTSD, like myself, have been prescribed a whole assortment of drugs by the VA, including Trazodone which was given to me as a sleep aid, but is commonly used as an anti-depressant even though clinical studies have shown that users have had increased suicidal thoughts while taking the drug. I no longer take Trazodone, but occasionally drink a little kava-kava to relieve anxiety, but others may find that medicinal herbs such as marijuana may be more useful in relieving stress and anxiety, but each individual is different and may have to go through a little trial and error before figuring out what works best for them.

Coping with PTSD is not easy and neither is getting the right type of help to treat it. People simply don't understand it. Some have preconceived notions about what it means to have it and treat those who are diagnosed with it in a special way because of these notions, and still others think PTSD is not a big deal and that combat veterans are no different than anyone else who has experienced a traumatic experience. New Mexico's law enforcement agencies and courts certainly haven't done very well with dealing with those who have PTSD and even doctors and psychiatrists who specialize in PTSD often don't know what is best for someone who is afflicted with the demon. I am still unsure what the best solution is for my PTSD, but know it is still an issue as I often become startled when I hear loud noises that sound like gunshots or explosions and sometimes I flinch when I drive over something that I think could be an IED, but somehow I can still dig myself out of any holes I've climbed into and get on with my day without much anguish. Others simply don't know where to turn for help and can't beat the triggers that go along with having PTSD which torment them every day.

There are so many triggers out there for a returning war veteran, and so many other issues to deal with that, coupled with the experiences of combat, can drive one over the edge. Family members and friends can add to the pressures one is already dealing with, while disasters, illness, and deaths of acquaintances and others can bring feelings of such pain that going on any longer just doesn't seem possible. Then there is the television, and the radio, and the newspapers which tell stories of further death, destruction, and deceit by government leaders, while giant billboards display images of dead bodies for some type of 'educational exhibit.' And then there is the dirt and the desert of New Mexico that brings back memories of Iraqi sandstorms and upturned dust from the long convoys of U.S. tanks and AAVs that caused such devastation on their way to the Tigris and Euphrates rivers. A piece of barbequed meat can trigger memories of the blackened bodies, many of which were women and children, that were strewn about the highway going through Nasariyah, and the smell of smoke can bring on feelings of panic after being reminded of a rocket attack back in Baghdad or it can kick one in to combat mode from the reminder of a gunfight they had been in. And it is this combat mode that makes PTSD for veterans so much different than PTSD for someone who has not been to war. When one goes into combat mode the whole body is affected. The heart rate beats faster, the mind starts to race, and something clicks on in the head that turns a usually normal human being into a killer - a killer who was trained to be just that by the United States government, but who, after leaving the service, is no longer trained in how to best channel one's killer traits.

The way a veteran deals with triggers and manages their combat mode mentality is what is so scary about the type of PTSD that afflicts them. One can turn the gun on themselves like ex-Marine and New Mexico native Diego Gonzales did last month after allegedly kidnapping his wife and children before being confronted by police, or one can become a vigilante and shoot someone else, as was the case of ex-Marine Elton John Richard who shot and killed Daniel Romero after he tried to break into his home back in 2008. Preventing these types of behaviors and treating veterans with PTSD is in the best interest of all of New Mexico and yesterday was the time to do something about it. I have advocated for a veterans' court, which we have seen some progress on with Sen. Eric Griego sponsoring a bill which calls for the study on the creation of such a court back in 2009, but not enough is being done. For me, leaving New Mexico made all the difference in the world, but some don't want to or don't have the means to leave the state, and they deserve the best help both private and public agencies can provide for warriors who return home with PTSD or any other wound, mental or physical, the wars in Iraq and Afghanistan (and elsewhere) have caused.

I was lucky to find a PTSD group at the Vet Center in Albuquerque which includes veterans of World War II, the Korean War, Vietnam, the Gulf War, and the Iraq and Afghan wars. The Vet Center is not the same as the VA hospital and it is much more accommodating. Services include group and one-on-one counseling, help receiving and understanding veterans' benefits, and it provides a great place to meet people of all ages who have to deal with a lot of the same issues other veterans have. The Vet Center may not be for everyone, and each person has their own way of dealing with their problems, but for those who have nowhere to turn I suggest starting at the Vet Center first. Other places to go include the VA hospital, the American Legion, the VFW, DAV, or other veterans association, a church group or meditation center, an herbalist or medicine man, or even an acupuncturist. No matter where one goes, what is important is that they are seeking help. I have found my peace of mind through writing and going to school and have been blessed with the opportunity to live in Hilo, HI, where, despite the constant sight and sound of low-flying Air Force jets, there really is an atmosphere of aloha and relaxation. For anyone else who is suffering with PTSD I hope you can find your peace of mind too, and for the country as a whole I hope our communities can come together to not only address the ongoing problem of PTSD, but to also take the necessary action to prevent future wars that can lead to an even greater psychological problem for this country.

Tue Jan 25, 2011 | 01:40 PM |

After Note: In the edited version published in *The Independent,* titled "A combat veteran's perspective on PTSD," the section discussing the triggers a war vet might have when seeing a piece of barbequed meat was omitted.[9] I wrote the following letter to the editor in protest which was published in the following issue of the paper on page 6.[10]

Graphic detail was needed in PTSD story

Last week The Independent published an article I wrote about my experiences with PTSD, which in my opinion brings attention to a very serious issue afflicting America. However a couple of sentences were edited out that I think should have remained. I'm not sure why the editor decided to delete one particularly important part of a sentence discussing the triggers of PTSD, but to me it is of utmost importance to let the public know what was missing. The sentence I'm talking about reads, "A piece of barbequed meat can trigger memories of the blackened bodies, many of which were women and children, that were strewn about the highway going through Nasiriya. . ."

Perhaps the editors think this is too gruesome of a description, or perhaps they are fearful of the response readers will have to this fact, or maybe there just wasn't enough space for everything I wrote. No matter the reason, I feel as though The Independent owes it to its readers to print this letter so the public can be better informed. The story about the innocent women and children who were killed in

Nasiriya and other parts of Iraq has to be told, not just because of the psychological consequences those deaths have had on soldiers returning home, but because it is the right thing to do. Most of the mainstream media has done little to provide details about the battle of Nasariya, and those who have, like the BBC, quote top-ranking officials to justify the deaths of innocent Iraqis saying they were using civilian shields, but I know this wasn't the case in all incidences. In one online BBC article titled "Nasiriya struggles with war memories" the British news service reports that around 1,000 Iraqis were killed during the fighting I witnessed in Nasiriya, most of them civilians.[11] This was one of the bloodiest battles of the war in Iraq, and yet little is known about what really happened there. If we don't talk about this we pave the way for it to happen again. If it wasn't for the photos of dead Jewish prisoners during the Holocaust of World War II, today's public would not have the evidence to support the facts regarding this slaughter, and if it wasn't for the photos taken during the Mai Lai massacre in Vietnam those who committed the crimes may never have been held accountable for their actions.

The truth, and the reporting of the truth, has to be known to prevent America from continuing its wartime policies of so called "justifiable killings" of innocent civilians which the military regularly calls collateral damage. It's easy for me to stand up to angry readers like one Edgewood resident who told me I had no right to feel guilty about the killing of these innocent people (after a previous article I wrote about my experiences in Iraq) because I'm half a world away and don't have to deal with these readers face to face, so to some degree I understand The Independent's decision not to print what I consider to be one of the most important parts of my article, but I'm still disappointed. That same Edgewood resident told me that he "bombed those [expletive]" in Iraq so somehow I am in the wrong for feeling bad about their deaths. I'm not wrong and neither are the other veterans who have stood up and voiced their opinion in newspapers like War Crimes Times and who have continued to protest the wars despite complete media blackouts about their activities.

This letter is not meant to criticize The Independent nor is meant to be anti-military or unpatriotic. In fact it is just the opposite. I give The Independent a pat on the back for giving me a voice to address veterans' issues like PTSD, and I am proud of our men and women in uniform who put their lives on the line for our freedom and safety. And, most importantly, I am a patriot in the truest of forms because I believe in and will stand up and fight for the Constitutional rights that grant me such democratic freedoms as the first amendment, which states that, "Congress shall make no law respecting an establishment of religion, or prohibiting the free exercise thereof; or abridging the freedom of speech, or of the press; or the right of the people peaceably to assemble, and to petition the Government for a redress of grievances." Because I am patriotic I will take advantage of this right and speak the truth to the public so that we can make more informed choices concerning the future of our country.
Scott Albright,
Iraq War Veteran 2003/2004
Hilo, Hawaii

The editor replies:
Scott Albright's story on PTSD was edited primarily to keep the piece to one topic, in this case PTSD in veterans. It was

shortened somewhat and graphic descriptions of war and violence were taken out. His letter is printed in its entirety.

The following was printed in the next issue of *The Independent*[12]:

Deleted portions were integral

Thank you for printing Scott Albright's article and letter. I've enjoyed his writing over the years, and am happy that he remains in contact with The Independent. I agree with Mr. Albright that the deleted portions of his article were an integral part of his story. Your editor says that this was done to "keep the piece to one topic" PTSD, Post Traumatic Stress Disorder. To delete the horrific scenes which Mr. Albright witnessed is to deny the reader important insight into the nature of PTSD. The image of masses of blackened bodies sickens me. What you call "graphic descriptions of war and violence" sicken me. But how else am I to understand these wars; how am I to empathize with those suffering with traumatic stress without those who have been there telling us their experiences? Who is going to tell me of the civilians killed, the parents and children, the teachers and merchants and bricklayers? Are we to forget or ignore that in war there is a great deal of tragedy and sorrow? Mr. Albright's letter goes on to explain and illustrate far better than I why this is so important; and I want to thank him for all he's done and for who he is. I hope that you are healing, Scott, and that you know that many of us support you in your patriotism, honesty and integrity. Please continue writing.
Marcia De Leon,
Edgewood

Solemn Note: One of the reasons I think it is so important to emphasize the number of innocent Iraqis killed in An-Nasiriyah during the invasion is because there has been a lack of mainstream media coverage of this part of the war. It is my belief that the "media" or imbedded reporters were misdirected from Nasiriyah by the whole Jessica Lynch fiasco. Of course I could always be wrong, but when doing a basic Google web search for the term 'An-Nasiriyah' only 1.5 million results are returned compared to the 6.5 million returns for the search term 'Jessica Lynch.' A Google News search for the period March 28, 2003 to April 5, 2003 using An-Nasiriyah as the search term returned results of news headlines and articles which provided very few details of the reality of the war, leaving the average news reader misinformed and without a reality-based visualization of what was going on in Nasiriyah at the time.

One *Spokesman-Review* headline read "Marines Blast a Path Through Nasiriyah," while *CBS News* ran the headline "On The Scene: Fighting for An-Nasiriyah," and in the *Sydney Morning Herald* the headline "Traffic's deadly on freeway to Baghdad" ran across the paper's pages. Of the dozen or so results showing up on the first page only one result caught my eye that seemed somewhat close to the reality I knew. On March 25, 2003 the *ioL news* ran the headline "Road to Baghdad 'littered with Iraqi bodies'," but the story only cites an AFP correspondent as saying "more than 100 Iraqi bodies littered the road north from Nasiriyah," a far cry from the 1,117 estimated deaths the Campaign for Innocent Victims in Conflict was quoted as saying in the above mentioned BBC article.[13]

The closest media account of what I saw in Nasiriyah came from a reporter named Mark Franchetti who was working for the pro-war paper *The Sunday Times* out of London. Franchetti goes into gruesome detail about the nightmarish onslaught of the city in the article titled "US Marines turn fire on civilians at the bridge of death", but access to the original article is for paying customers only.[14] A website titled redandgreen.org reprints much of the article online, providing its own commentary on the details, but many might dismiss the website all together because it is not a well known "reputable" news media outlet, but I can assure you that what Franchetti is quoted as reporting is very accurate. An article in the *NewStatesman* titled "We are the chemotherapy" also comments on Franchetti's article, providing an interesting perspective to the war that I could not and was not allowed to see when I was in Iraq. Unfortunately what the *NewStatesman* tells us is that despite the fact that many people share the same anti-war perspective, a U.S. led war in Iran and Syria could very well be just as inevitable as the war in Iraq was. I certainly hope not.

From Autocracy to Militancy to Democracy

The first thing I thought about when I saw the video of protesters in Cairo is that they needed to get the military on their side. Sure enough protesters were kissing soldiers, shaking their hands, and riding on their vehicles, but there were no signs that the military was going to do the dirty work of the protesters. They remained neutral and the protesters seemed to do little to get them to move against pro-Mubarak thugs at first. Eventually Mubarak stepped down and passed on his power to the military, which is now in firm control of the country, but the work of the protesters is still incomplete. The military has said there will be a smooth transition to civilian rule with the promise of free and open elections, which sounds great, and hopefully will work out for the Egyptian people, but we cannot stop here. Much work needs to be done to ensure the military will allow civilian control of the country to resume. Yes, the current situation is better than allowing Mubarak to stay in power, but Egyptians need to continue to be wary of a government controlled by generals and conscripts, as military rule is about as far from democracy as the moon is from earth. I am optimistic that a coalition of opposition members will work directly with the military to ensure that the rule of law will be implemented in a fair and just manner during this period of transition, and am hopeful that free elections will produce the type of leadership that Egypt needs to provide for its people and be a thriving member of the international community. This optimism should not be laced with naivety however. Opposition members need to embed themselves into the offices currently being held in all levels of government with the expectation that those offices will be later filled by government representatives chosen by the people.

The lesson learned from Egypt is important for all the potential hot spots across the region, and the planet. In Libya we see a semi-split within the military between opposition and government forces and in other parts of the region the pressure is certainly on members of the military to choose sides, but mutiny or an all out military junta is not the best solution for democracy to arise. Opposition forces who truly want democracy not only need to win the military over, but they need to convince them that civilian control of the military is the best path for a peaceful transition to occur. Things are already out of control in Libya and the death toll keeps climbing, while Yemen and Bahrain are also experiencing harsh crackdowns that make it appear that a peaceful revolution is out of the question. I pray for the sake of the people that peace is still an available option, and I contend that winning over the military is the best way to go about it, but doing that will not be easy. How that can be done when officers' loyalty has been to the autocratic leaders of these countries for decades is a tough problem indeed, but through organizational planning, direct talks between opposition members and the military, and fast and furious campaigns through word of mouth, telephone conversations, texts and emails, it can be done.

No matter who is in the forefront of these revolutionary movements the United States needs to throw their support behind them because democracy is not and should never be on the side of authoritarianism. The U.S. has supported corrupt dictators for far too long, and now is the chance for the country to prove that its foreign policy is not as hypocritical as it is perceived to be across the planet. By supporting the removal of autocrats across the globe the U.S. can prove that it is true to its word when it says democracy has its place in all countries. Sure there is the potential for blowback by supporting opposition movements as not all democracies provide a majority that is pro-American, but the continued support of leaders who deem themselves all powerful by decree of god also has the potential to cause severe problems for America. I do not think covert support is the right answer either, as secrecy is the opposite of transparency, which is a true marking of democracy. What is important to remember is that guns alone cannot win the battle. It's the voice of the people that counts the most, and the people want freedom. Martin Luther King Jr. said it best when he said let freedom ring because, in his own words, "when this happens, when we allow freedom to ring, when we let it ring from every village and every hamlet, from every state and every city, we will be able to speed up that day when all of God's children, black men and white men, Jews and Gentiles, Protestants and Catholics, will be able to join hands and sing in the words of the old Negro spiritual, "Free at last! free at last! thank God Almighty, we are free at last!" And that is all the people want - to be free at last. Free from oppression, free from the laws of stubborn old men, and free from the chaos that ensues when madmen are allowed to stay in power for too long.

Mon Feb 21, 2011 | 10:20 AM |

Supporting Uprisings without Empowering Extremism
    The recent uprisings throughout the Middle East and North Africa are both cause for concern and cause for optimism in the United States. On the one hand American leaders are unsure who the protesters are that are demanding the end of autocratic regimes in the region, and many are afraid the popular movements are fueled by extremism and anti-Americanism, while on the other hand leaders see an opportunity for democracy to take root in an area where nepotism, corruption, and dictatorship has ruled for way too long. No one can be sure if the so-called democracy movements are really aspiring to be democratic, and even if they are it's not clear whether the majority of the people will be friendly to America and its allies, yet the United States has an obligation to support the rule of the people by the people everywhere in the world. Unfortunately this has not been the case. The U.S. has provided military, political, and economic support to the autocratic governments in Yemen, Saudi Arabia, Egypt, and Bahrain for many years, and in turn these

countries have helped the U.S. capture terrorists and transnational criminals while giving American forces a place to stage military and intelligence operations in the region. In Yemen the U.S. is in a precarious situation as al-Qaeda, anti-government separatists, and other extremists have been operating there for some time and it is almost certain these elements are taking part in the opposition movement we see there today. This seems like a good enough reason to continue providing military and intelligence support to the ruling party led by President Ali Abdullah Saleh who has held the top post since 1994, but it is not.

The U.S. needs to stick to its principals and support a leadership that is willing to be led by the people, not one which does not listen to its people. So who should the U.S. support then if there is no other political party or faction that can assist the U.S. in the same way Saleh has? The answer: no one. Not to say the U.S. should abandon ship, cut off ties, and let the country slip into civil war and become a failed state. This does not serve American, or the world's, interests. Right now is the time to provide institution strengthening, heavy international diplomatic pressure, and a barrage of information dissemination, as these are the mechanisms that will lead toward a long term peace. Political or military support to one faction or the other may serve someone's interests, somewhere, in the short term, but it hasn't proven to work in favor for the rest of the world over the long term.

So far the U.S. military support to opposition forces in Libya has not proven to be successful in ending the violence, creating democratic reform, or causing Qaddafi to cave in and quit his post. What this proves is that military might does not make everything right, however ending violence in a timely fashion without the use of more violence has been a problem for policymakers since the dawn of civilization, and obviously there are no easy answers. That doesn't mean there aren't any at all.

Providing the tools and technical assistance needed to strengthen both public and private institutions is the first step toward building a long term peace, not only in the places where blood is being spilled today, but also in places where the potential for violence looms at all times. The U.S. cannot do this alone, but it can lead the international community in the right direction. Much focus has been given to providing military and intelligence support and police training, while less attention has been given to areas like crime prevention, social equality, and community building. There are institutions that provide services in these forgotten areas, and it is not hard to see that these institutions are weak, not only in the troubled areas around the globe, but even in the rich industrialized countries that are supposed to be directing the world toward peace, cooperation, and harmonious living.

Institution building takes time, but the process can be moved along faster with the right funding, the right leaders, and the right approach, and now is the time to set the wheels in motion. This is where the international community can step in. The G-8 countries can provide the funding, the World Bank the tools, and the U.N. can provide the leaders. Specialists in crime prevention, conflict and post-conflict resolution, and government and economic reforms need to form a leaders' group that can identify the institutions that need to be strengthened or built from scratch in the most troubled areas like Yemen and Libya and then gain access to the areas that are safe to work, send in the teams that are capable and willing, and then begin the process of activating their skills. Training locals can take place immediately while actual supplies need not be extravagant. A crime prevention or conflict resolution specialist need not work out of an expensive building - a shack will do just fine. Once teams are in place - and yes security will be needed and NATO is probably the most capable of providing it - then the message must be disseminated for the process to spread into the troubled areas. This is where public relations specialists and media organizations come in.

It is up to the journalists, who are always so quick to get on the ground in war zones and uprisings, to spread the word. Journalists tend to only bring images of violence and stories of rebel movements and government responses back to their viewers in countries far away from where the action is. Journalists are good at this and are not public relations officers, but they know how to get into the thick of things, so they are best suited for this job. Their mission should not be to just report back to their bosses what they see on the ground, it is also their job to let the locals know that action is being taken in areas other than just the front lines. They can disseminate the information provided by the specialists strengthening and building institutions and they can let the locals know that their input is needed, especially in the areas of government and economic reform - and that there are specialists in country willing to help, with the condition that only peaceful measures will be considered. Disseminating this information should not be that hard. Printing gazillions of flyers, newsletters and newspapers, pamphlets and other documents is not too costly and getting them in country and spread around is much easier than distributing medical and food supplies. A little creativity could go a long way in this respect, but even more so when trying to apply technological innovations. Cell phones can also be passed out that can provide real time updates to those on the ground. Portable giant digital billboards can be erected to display video and text messages from the international community wishing to provide the information about humanitarian aid, medical, and institutional services that are available. Through cell phones and computers, which can be easily disseminated, although maybe not as easy as pamphlets, dialogue between the international community, local government leaders, opposition groups, and members of the military can be created. Direct communication can go a long way in preventing further violence and can help lessen rumors and misinformation from creating more havoc.

Of course this begs the questions of who should be directing the communication, where does the military and intelligence community fit into this, and how should medical supplies, clean water, food, and long-term economic and political support be placed into the equation. Well I'll leave that part for another time, because right now no one in the U.S., or in the international community for that matter, seem to sense the type of urgency needed to address these issues right now, so time is on the side of those who have it made in the shade, but perhaps someone who doesn't have the privilege of having so much time to not worry about the next wave of violence will read this and start taking action on their own.

Sun Apr 3, 2011 | 03:15 PM |

A Concoction for the 21st Century: Patriotism, Globalization, and Multiculturalism

Two great things happened to me recently which made me seriously consider my position on what it means to be a patriot in a world of multinational corporations, pan-regional government policies, international terrorism, and the global digital information age. The first great thing that happened is I won a scholarship from AT&T that is given to military veterans each year. In order to win I had to write an essay explaining why I am a patriot. The essay should be posted on the scholarship website sometime soon, just click on this link1 to take a peek and see if it's up yet. The other great thing that happened is I had my first academic journal article published in the Yishu Journal of Contemporary Chinese Art.[15] The journal article explains how Chinese artist Xu Bing used the ashes from the fallen World Trade Center after 9/11 to produce a poem in which he asks 'As there is nothing from the first, Where does the dust itself collect?' Throughout my article I explain the importance of cross-cultural exchanges and the use of art as a tool for shaping a more peaceful society. I state that it is closed minded to be nationalistic and then explain how the world is too interconnected for us as humans to continue thinking that one country, culture, or lifestyle is better than another. Nationalism feeds violence, and we are all affected by any violence which upholds this notion that one group is greater than another, no matter where we live in the world. To some this may seem contradictory to my essay on patriotism in which I explain why the United States is so great and why I am proud to be from the U.S., however this is not a contradiction it is simply an affirmation of my beliefs.

As Joseph Nye explains in *The Paradox of American Power*, one of the reasons the U.S. has been so successful in spreading "western" ideologies in an era of fast paced globalization is that the U.S. is such a mix of cultures, both borrowed and original, that the American way has become universal in the sense that people from all over the world can relate to it.[16] Of course the rest of the world can't truly experience the American way of life through the commercial exportation of culture, they must really experience it themselves to understand it, however exported American culture can provide a small sample of what the country has to offer. For me being proud of the American way and being patriotic for my country doesn't mean being ethnocentric or taking the belief that the U.S. is better than every other country. No, being patriotic is quite the opposite. It means being accepting of every other culture and way of life in the world and knowing that Americans can absorb these ways and weave them into the global fabric of society for the entire world to enjoy. Being patriotic means knowing that the U.S. is a cross-cultural blend of the entire human race and that American values are the world's values. So when you are reading my essay on patriotism and my article on Xu Bing don't look for the contradictions between patriotism and trans-nationalism, look for the affirmations that show how I am a patriot living in a borderless world where trans-nationalism and global citizenry are just as American as apple pie and baseball.

Fri Sep 9, 2011 | 08:16 AM |

After Note: The following is the essay I wrote for the AT&T veteran's scholarship for which I was awarded first prize. AT&T never did publish it on their website even though other winners' essays were published there in the past. I'm not sure why they didn't, but I decided to add it here because I think it is pretty good, and it's an honest reflection of how I feel. On that note: It is my hope the images and words I provided within these pages are not seen as being propagandistic, nationalistic, or in any way promoting war or violence, but neither are they anti-American, anti-military, or meant as an insult to those who have risked their time, energy, and sometimes lives to make the United States, and the world, a better place for all.

I Am A Patriot – Here's Why

The United States of America is the land of liberty. It is a place like no other where people from all over the world come together to live free of oppression and the rule by authoritarian regimes. It is a place where the government is formed by the people for the people. It is the home of the free, the brave, and the diverse. It is a place where different cultures flourish and grow, where people practice whatever religion they choose, and where ideological differences are settled civilly without dividing and fragmenting the country, but rather by strengthening and uniting it further. This is the U.S.A., and this my country. I am proud to be a part of it and honored to have served in the military to protect it. This is why I love the United States, and this is why I am a patriot.

While serving in Iraq as a United States Marine I fought for the ideals and principals of liberty and freedom. I helped to remove Saddam Hussein from power - a dictator who is so ruthless he gassed and killed his own people for standing up for freedom. While in Iraq I stood side by side in uniform with men and women from as far away as Florida and the Alaskan frontier who also believed in the principles of liberty and freedom. We fought together not as whites, blacks, Hispanics, Asians, and Indians, but as Americans united in a battle against the enemies who want to divide us and strip us of our liberties. Together we fought for our families and friends back home, we fought to preserve the American way of life, and we fought for our leaders who we all had the privilege of electing into office to represent our beliefs and ideas. The fact that so many different ideas are represented in our leadership, and that the people who believe in these different ideas are willing to come together and voluntarily fight for them is what makes this country so great. This is why I'm proud to have served in uniform, and this is why I am a patriot.

The three hundred and fifty million Americans living in the United States are not just a diverse group of races, religions, and cultures, but they are a diverse population of thinkers. They are a population of artists and laborers, business owners and politicians, firemen and teachers, and engineers and electricians. They are a population of athletes and celebrities, doctors and lawyers, organizers and volunteers. They are a population of people who can be whatever they want because in the United States anyone can make it if they try. More importantly, everyone has the ability to shape the future of the country to ensure the next generation of Americans makes it even better. The brilliant minds of Americans help to write history every day, and they do it all over the world. From Europe to Asia, South America to Africa - people from across the globe look to the United States for inspiration on how to make their country better, how to improve their businesses, and how to make their schools, hospitals, and public and private institutions look more like America's. This is because the diversity of American thought and ingenuity created a system the world likes and wants as their own. This is because Americans are leaders who are unafraid of trying new things, and because they are courageous enough to cross thresholds no one else dares to cross. This is what makes America great, and this is why I am a patriot.

No matter where I go in the world and no matter what language people speak, there's always a common thread in the conversations I hear, and that is the desire of people to be free. To have freedom of thought, speech, and action - to have the freedom to speak their minds about their own feelings and beliefs, and to be free to share these feelings with whomever they please. Unfortunately not every place on earth allows for these freedoms, but luckily for me I do live in a place that not only allows these freedoms, but guarantees their protection through the law. Like many other Americans I am proud of the system we have that allows for such freedoms, and like many other Americans I am proud to share these freedoms with the rest of the world. From the Spring Revolutions of the Middle East and North Africa to the Color Revolutions of Central Asia and Eastern Europe, people call for more liberty because they also want to be able to share the type of freedoms America has to offer. In China imprisoned youth write and think about how to make their country more democratic and free, while in parts of Africa impoverished mothers and fathers look to the United States for ways to be more prosperous and happy. The United States is the beacon in the night, it is the shining city on a hill, and it is the guiding post for the rest of the world to follow. This is my country - a country of hope and opportunity, a country of happiness and prosperity, a country of benevolence and greatness. This is my country, and this is why I am a patriot.

CHAPTER 6 NOTES

[1] The link to the wartime contracting hearing discussed in this post is no longer active. It had earlier been made available on c-span.org. It may still be available via the c-span video library hidden somewhere in their archives. To download the Commission on Wartime Contracting final report to congress, *Transforming Wartime Contracting* (August 2011), visit www.wartimecontracting.gov.

[2] Farah, Douglas and Stephen Braun. *Merchant of Death*. Hoboken, N.J.: John Wiley & Sons, 2007.

[3] Ibid.

[4] See USIP webpage, "Ambassador Christopher Hill on the Next Chapter in Iraq," Event Summary. http://www.usip.org/events/ambassador-christopher-hill-the-next-chapter-in-iraq.

[5] C-Span Video Library. *Future Operations in Iraq,* U.S. Institute of Peace, online video (1 hour, 33 minutes), August. 18, 2010. http://www.c-spanvideo.org/program/295091-1.

[6] Perkins, John. *The Secret History of the American Empire: Economic Hit Men, Jackals, and the Truth About Global Corruption*. New York: Penguin Group, 2007

[7] U.S. Defense Department. *Military and Security Developments Involving the People's Republic of China 2010,* Annual Report to Congress, 2010. http://www.defense.gov/pubs/pdfs/2010_CMPR_Final.pdf.

[8] Proactive Investors. "Boeing and PetroChina to assess setting up Chinese aviation-biofuels industry," May 27, 2010. http://www.proactiveinvestors.com/companies/news/6197.

[9] http://www.the-independent-newspaper.com/images/weeklypdf/independent011911.pdf

[10] http://www.the-independent-newspaper.com/images/weeklypdf/independent012611.pdf

[11] North, Andrew. "Nasiriya struggles with war memories," *BBC News,* June 17, 2003. http://news.bbc.co.uk/2/hi/middle_east/2995568.stm.

[12]*The Independent,* p. 6. http://www.the-independent-newspaper.com/images/weeklypdf/independent020211.pdf.

[13] ioL News. "Road to Baghdad 'littered with bodies'," March 25, 2003. http://www.iol.co.za/news/world/road-to-baghdad-littered-with-iraqi-

bodies-1.103222#.UL8gaoNTySo.

[14] Franchetti, Mark. "US Marines turn fire on civilians at bridge of death," *The Sunday Times,* March 30, 2003. http://www.thesundaytimes.co.uk/sto/news/world_news/article45515.ece.

[15] Albright, Scott. "Xu Bing: Transcending Culture," *Yishu Journal of Contemporary Chinese Art* (2011). http://yishu-online.com/browse-articles/?488.

[16] Nye, Joseph S., Jr. *The Paradox of American Power, Why the World's Only Superpower Can't Go it Alone.* New York: Oxford University Press, 2002.

WWW.VETERANSNOTES.WEEBLY.COM

www.ingramcontent.com/pod-product-compliance
Lightning Source LLC
Chambersburg PA
CBHW070009300526
45794CB00001B/257